Kitty Grub

Cooking made easy for your cat

RUDY EDALATI

BALBOA.
PRESS
A DIVISION OF HAY HOUSE

Balboa Press books may be ordered through booksellers or by contacting:

Balboa Press
A Division of Hay House
1663 Liberty Drive
Bloomington, IN 47403
www.balboapress.com
1 (877) 407-4847

Because of the dynamic nature of the Internet, any web addresses or
links contained in this book may have changed since publication and
may no longer be valid. The views expressed in this work are solely those
of the author and do not necessarily reflect the views of the publisher,
and the publisher hereby disclaims any responsibility for them.

The author of this book does not dispense medical advice or prescribe the use
of any technique as a form of treatment for physical, emotional, or medical
problems without the advice of a physician, either directly or indirectly. The
intent of the author is only to offer information of a general nature to help
you in your quest for emotional and spiritual well-being. In the event you use
any of the information in this book for yourself, which is your constitutional
right, the author and the publisher assume no responsibility for your actions.

Any people depicted in stock imagery provided by Thinkstock are models,
and such images are being used for illustrative purposes only.
Certain stock imagery © Thinkstock.

Print information available on the last page.

ISBN: 978-1-4525-9895-6 (sc)
ISBN: 978-1-4525-9897-0 (hc)
ISBN: 978-1-4525-9896-3 (e)

Library of Congress Control Number: 2014920549

Balboa Press rev. date: 2/5/2015

This book is dedicated to

The cat that keeps their human protected
against vermin and the threat of disease
The dog that has always protected their
human from harm and loneliness
The horse that has carried and fought in
battle alongside their human

And to my Mamazoid
And my Princess Pooty, RIP

Contents

Introduction

It is common today to see cats living as companion animals with people all over the world. However, it is only recently that the animal we now know as the domesticated cat first came to live side by side with human beings. On the grander scale of evolution, it may be fair to say that cats are barely domesticated, so similar are they to their wild feline cousins. Their nutritional needs have certainly not strayed from their carnivorous roots.

I have many cats myself, and I often foster cats that are ill. I have had many cats come through my door over the years, healthy and frail, young and old. Despite their background, one thing I know for certain is that cats thrive on stimulation, good food, and loads of love and affection.

The one very special cat I have is Pooty. She is a very old puss and has been with me for over nineteen years. As she was already an adult cat when I met her, my guess is that she is in her early twenties. Yet a retired old puss she is not; she is as sprightly as ever, enjoying life by eating well and sleeping ninety percent of her days. I believe the success of her longevity may be attributed to the fact that I have never fed her commercial cat food. Her favorite food has always been chicken.

Pooty has been my guinea pig since the beginning of my pet food business. She is pretty finicky about what she likes, so she has been the perfect little cat food taster and head of my recipe approval committee. If Pooty will eat it, I know it must be good.

When it comes to cats, the most important thing to remember is that by nature they are desert animals. Having originated from desert climates, cats should rarely drink water in excess. Most of the fluid they consume should come from the food they're ingesting. Commercial cat foods are typically very dry, containing surplus salt and minerals. This, in turn, makes animals on this type of diet go against their nature and drink water in large amounts.

In its natural environment a cat in the wild would kill its prey, then eat its stomach, organs, and bodily fluids. A veritable one-stop nutrition shop. I have seen my own cats killing small mammals such as rabbits and squirrels. I have observed that the cats seek first to eat the head of their prey, filling up on the goodness that this body part provides.

Often, a headless carcass tells me that the cat has had its fill of nutrition and has no interest in finishing the remainder of its prey, regardless of how bountiful a meal it may still be. Cats also like to eat a variety of bugs, which, in my opinion, are some of the best sources of protein a cat can get. As unappealing as it may sound to us, for a cat a nice juicy creepy crawly is just the ticket for a fill of protein.

Let's allow cats to get back to some nutritional nature basics. Cooking for cats is very easy and rewarding —both economically for you and nutritionally for your pet, as you are in complete control of what your cat is ingesting. Many health issues can be effectively controlled with an informed and proper diet. Good food for your cat equals good health. I don't believe any medical therapy can achieve optimum benefits without an adjustment of the patient's diet to aid in the goal.

On my property in rural Maryland, I have an abundance of animals: nine dogs, eight cats, three horses, and a variety of geese, ducks, and chickens. I share my thirty acres with them readily, knowing that they are stimulated, exercised, and able to experience the joy of living as close as possible to what Mother Nature intended for them.

I cook for all my dogs and cats. My beloved animal companions are a testament to what good wholesome nutrition can do. Let's consider my cats: Pooty, as I have already mentioned, is the eldest and at least twenty-three. Then comes the rest of the brood (many of whom you'll read about later in this book), including Kat Ashley at the ripe old age of fourteen. Following her is Edgar, at thirteen and a half, and then Cheeba, six months younger, at thirteen. Amber follows at the age of twelve, with Honey is at least nine and Cagney is not far behind, at around eight years of age. Spider, my youngest puss, comes in at about a year old.

As you can see, my cats are living long and living large! I absolutely believe that my home-cooked food has helped promote their generous life spans. I also know that with continued quality nutrition they'll thrive for years to come, enriching my life with their loving companionship and unconditional loyalty and affection.

My goal in this book is to simplify the subject of cat nutrition and make feeding your feline companions an occasion of daily joy and satisfaction.

Historically, people almost everywhere have fed their cats home-cooked food, whether specifically intended for them or offered as discarded leftovers from the dweller's own meals. Cats have come this far alongside humans in the evolutionary process. Let's see how much further into the future they will come with us if we use our common sense and well-informed nutrition and cooking practices. I invite anyone who wants what's best for their feline to join with me in cooking for their cats.

CHAPTER 1

The Cat Connection: Diet and Health

W hat's the first thing you think of when you think "cat food"? I'm sure the first thing you thought of was canned "wet" food or dry kibble.

The dry kibble that the world generally perceives as cat food is by far the worst thing to feed cats. It is extremely important to understand that cats have a minimal amount of taste buds, even fewer taste buds than dogs possess. Therefore, it is really their sense of smell that motivates a cat to eat.

Processed Cat Food

Processed food is less fresh than food that is specially prepared at home and eaten shortly after cooking. Any food product that goes into a can or a bag to be sold off the shelf in a store must be preserved, and the wholesomeness of such a product must be called into question. If it is chemically preserved, you have to wonder about how safe those chemicals are for your animal to ingest. For these reasons it is much better to cook at home and make fresh food. Homemade cat food can be prepared ahead and frozen or kept fresh refrigerated for the week to come.

Preservatives can build up in the body over time and pollute the digestive system, thereby interfering with the normal functions of organs that maintain good health and cleanse the body, such as the liver and kidneys. This buildup happens much faster in smaller animals than in humans. Other probably hazards include liver damage, fetal abnormalities, and thyroid dysfunction.

Questionable Ingredients

Who really knows what's in processed food? You never have to wonder if you make your cat's meals yourself, since you can eliminate unwanted and harmful ingredients from your cat's diet. When reading the labels on brand-name cat food containers, it's not always easy to identify the ingredients mentioned. What is a meat byproduct or a chicken byproduct? What about animal digest? These are ingredients that would not sound so healthy called by their correct names. Pet food companies are not obliged to list all the ingredients that go into their products, and oftentimes the ingredients listed on the labels go by names that the ordinary consumer cannot recognize.

The pet food industry is not regulated by the government in the same way that the Food and Drug Administration (FDA) regulates food designated for human consumption. The industry has a self-regulatory board, the American Association of Feed Control Officials (AAFCO), which defines the nutritional, testing, and labeling requirements for processed pet food. As recent media attention has demonstrated, when standards are not as rigid and companies not as accountable, casualties will eventually occur. Numerous reports of pet deaths have occurred due to contaminated ingredients found in commercial pet foods. As tragic as these deaths are, they highlight how questionable the production process of commercial pet food really is. If you cannot identify what the ingredients are and how they got to their current state, how can you knowingly offer them to your beloved companion animal?

The pet food industry is a big, highly competitive, and hugely profitable business; therefore, cat food companies keep their recipes and preparation processes closely guarded secrets. Because we don't know exactly what pet food companies do to process their cat food, we can only trust that they don't overcook it, robbing it of essential nutrients. When foods are too overcooked, which might be done to sterilize their contents, for example, they lose much of their nutritional value. The minerals are processed out of them so they must then be artificially supplemented. Many of the ingredients on pet food labels are synthetic nutrients added back into the processed food.

Processed cat foods now are also marketed toward age categories, such as kittens or seniors, and for the management of specific ailments. No matter what is on the label, however, proper nutrition is a highly individualized balance of requirements dictated by genetics, age, and health status. Of course, cat food manufacturers do conduct feeding and digestibility research trials, but the bottom line is that one kind of cat food is not going to be good for all cats.

In recent years, the general public and the medical establishment have begun to accept and readily advocate nutrition as one of the most powerful tools we have available to create optimal health for ourselves. It is the cornerstone of preventive care and healing. Adages have honored this truth for centuries ("An apple a day keeps the doctor away"). Today, many cat lovers are beginning to apply the same holistic approach to pet nutrition. Why not? It's such a simple solution.

While it may be commonly recognized that there are everyday benefits to feeding your cat processed food, such as speed and convenience, and the more mythical benefits of "scientifically formulated" recipes for complete nutrition, these are far outweighed by the detriments that the processing of cat food offers your pet's health in the long term.

Feeding Practices

Interestingly, I have come to observe a bizarre phenomenon accelerating at a rapid rate: obsessive compulsive behavior in cats. Specifically, overeating and an apparent addiction to dry cat food.

I have noticed that many cats appear to be addicted to dry cat food, as though they can't get enough of it. In every case the people of the household leave dry cat food out all day, essentially for their cat to "graze." This is the most unnatural thing owners could do for their feline companions.

Cats are not grazing animals, like cattle or horses. They are hunters, and as such there must always be a feed schedule for them to follow. Grazing throughout the day will almost certainly cause health and weight issues for cats who are fed this way. While it may seem convenient for you, it is definitely not ideal for your puss.

So many ailments in cats today can be directly attributed to poor nutrition or incorrect feeding, both responsibilities of the cat owner. Such ailments include diabetes mellitus, obesity, urinary tract infections, inflammatory bowel disease, and thyroid disorders.

Leslie Taylor, DVM, of Canal Clinic in Potomac, Maryland, states that over 59 percent of her cat patients may develop diabetes due to food and nutrition issues. In these cases she recommends her feline patients be put on the Atkins diet, where protein is the primary source of nutrients being ingested.

Dr. Taylor also suggests that if cats are on a more suitable diet, such as the Atkins diet, their diabetes can in fact be reversed, and the need for insulin will be erased. Interestingly, another possible trigger for diabetes suggested by Dr. Taylor may be the use of cortisone in treating cats for a variety of other health problems.

A common complaint of many cat owners is urinary tract issues for their puss. Many of us have suffered the aroma of a cat that has urinated or sprayed around the house. For many cat owners it may appear to be a behavioral issue, but many times the root of the problem is, in fact, physiological —directly linked to the animal's diet. It appears to be a significant problem in neutered male cats but also occurs in female cats both spayed and unspayed.

Here again, we must take into account that cats absolutely need fluid in their diet. When eating primarily dry food, cats have the essential juices needed in their diet taken away. This, in addition to excess stress, can often trigger cystitis. In order to avoid these health problems, the alternative of cooking for your feline pet offers all the goodness that comes from fresh, natural, juicy protein sources.

Kidney disease is also an extremely prevalent problem in cats, according to Dr. Taylor. Many cats will develop kidney disease in older age. The treatment for kidney disease is relatively controversial. In the past, many people believed that by limiting protein in the cat's diet, their kidney function would improve. However, often the excess supplements contained in commercial pet food can be counterproductive. Pure protein from a home-cooked diet would be much more effective.

Cats are carnivores. They need two to three times more protein —meat protein —than omnivores such as dogs or humans. Cats have evolved in such a way that their kidneys are able to handle the large amounts of nitrogen produced from this protein. Exactly why is still being studied, but it is fair to say that for a cat with kidney disease, it is appropriate to have a higher amount of protein rather than reduced amount. More, in this instance, is definitely better. Therefore, adding protein-rich eggs or flaxseed oil is necessary when modifying the diet of a cat with kidney problems.

Flaxseed oil has many beneficial nutritional qualities. Primarily, it acts as a cleanser for the small glands in the kidneys, called the glomeruli. When these glands stop working and waste does not get effectively filtered, kidney problems arise. However, a dose of flaxseed added to a cat's diet each day helps clean the glomeruli so that efficient and healthy kidney function is restored.

Deborah Zoran, DVM, PhD DACVIM, even suggests in her article "The Carnivore Connection to Nutrition in Cats" (*JAVMA*, December 1, 2002) that cats must have a higher basal requirement for nitrogen than other animals, or at least an increased requirement for essential amino acids. This means that cats simply need a high level of meat protein, an absolute necessity in their daily diet, more so than other animals.

Cats have the potential to become anorexic and start losing muscle mass if they are not fed an adequate meat protein diet. Unlike a dog, for instance, which will draw on fat stored in the body, cats need a sustained intake of protein in order to maintain a healthy body mass.

A cat's system continues to need protein and its metabolic rate remains constant despite any inadequacies in its diet or state of inactivity. In a cat that is meat protein deficient, the body will take protein from its muscle mass. Therefore its body may appear extremely thin, as if wasting away.

In summary, for optimum nutrition, it is essential to consider the origins of a cat's diet and replicate it as closely as possible in the domesticated setting. Many illnesses occur in cats when people buy into commercially marketed diets rather than look to common sense and nature for what a cat needs nutritionally.

Not only will the animal benefit from quality, naturally wholesome, and nutritious food, but the cat owner can have peace of mind knowing that what their beloved yet genetically wild feline is eating is actually good—and safe—for them.

CHAPTER 2

Cat Nutrition 101

A cat's caloric needs depend on its age and health status. If you have an old, frail cat, for instance, it would need a higher caloric intake and higher protein intake than a young kitten or healthy adult cat. The protein intake of a very sick animal could go as high as 90 percent of its total calories each day.

Macronutrients

Foods that must be eaten in large quantities are called macronutrients. Macro means "big." The macronutrients are protein, carbohydrates, and fat. They have been called the building blocks of life. During digestion, enzymes in the juices of the stomach and intestines chemically dissolve foods, making it possible for the body to absorb and use the available nutrients. The macronutrients participate in, and fuel, numerous metabolic functions that keep all things alive and healthy.

Protein

Cats must eat more protein than any other type of food. Protein supplies amino acids, which are the infrastructure of the body.

It is used to build and maintain muscle mass and helps regulate hormones and brain chemicals. If a cat does not eat enough protein, its body begins to take protein from the existing lean muscle mass, weakening the animal. There are two types of protein: complete proteins and combined proteins.

Protein is composed of bonds of twenty-two amino acids in various combinations. Some of these amino acids are manufactured within a cat's body, so they do not have to be ingested. Others, however, must be taken from food. The second kind are called essential amino acids and include valine, leucine, isoleucine, threonine, methionine, phenylalanine, tryptophan, histidine, arginine, and lysine. The quality of a protein is directly related to the number and amount of essential amino acids it contains.

Complete proteins are those foods that supply all the essential amino acids in sufficient amounts. These are found in eggs, meat, fish, and dairy products, such as milk and cheese. Soy is the only plant-based complete protein. However, I do not advocate feeding soy to cats, because it would not be available to them naturally in the wild. Therefore their bodies are not genetically predisposed to digest it.

Incomplete proteins are foods that are missing several amino acids. Sources of incomplete proteins include legumes, whole grains, nuts, and seeds. To satisfy the body's need for amino acids, these must be eaten in combination with others. When two or more plant-based proteins are eaten in combination, they can create a complete protein. For example, rice and beans create a complete protein. Cereals such as oats and barley are very low in amino acids.

Amino Acids

There are eleven amino acids that cats cannot synthesize, or produce, themselves. Therefore it is absolutely essential that your kitty receive them through its daily diet. In addition, an important point to note is that the amounts needed of taurine, arginine, methionine, and cystine are higher in cats than in dogs or other animals.

The eleven essential amino acids are

➢ arginine
➢ hestidine
➢ isolucine
➢ leucine
➢ lysine
➢ methionine
➢ phenylalanine
➢ taurine
➢ threonine
➢ trytophan
➢ valine

Non-essential amino acids include

➢ alanine
➢ asparagine
➢ aspartate
➢ cysteine***
➢ carnitine***
➢ glutamate
➢ glysine
➢ glutamine***
➢ proline
➢ serine
➢ tyrosine*** —*Important for melanin deficiencies (when black haired cats turn reddish-brown)*

*** Conditionally essential—not recognized by the AAFCO as essential, but research suggests that it is.

Carbohydrates

Cats need a much lower intake of carbohydrates than other animals. They lack an enzyme necessary to digest carbohydrates. Since cats are hunters, or predators, they would receive enough carbohydrates to fulfill their limited nutritional needs from their prey. Furthermore, since cats are carnivores, too much carbohydrate in their diets can decrease protein digestibility.

All vegetables, fruits, cereals, and grains contain carbohydrates. Carbohydrates include everything that isn't fat, protein, or water. Carbohydrates supply instant energy. Although protein and fat provide sustained energy, those are sources of reserved calories locked into muscles and organs. Surplus carbohydrates are generally stored as fat for the body's future use in cases of famine.

There are two types of carbohydrates: simple and complex.

Simple carbohydrates include table sugar (sucrose), which your cat does not need, fruit sugar (fructose), and milk sugar (lactose). Fruit provides fiber, vitamins, and minerals, along with energy. Milk provides protein and fat along with energy. Starchy vegetables or roots, such as potato, sweet potato, carrots, turnips, and beets, contain simple carbohydrates in combination with other essential nutrients.

Complex carbohydrates are composed of longer strands of sugar molecules and come from vegetables, legumes (beans, lentils, and peas), and whole grains, such as wheat and barley. Complex carbohydrates are the most ideal carbohydrates to consume because they metabolize quickly and contain essential nutrients.

Unlike protein, the more you cook carbohydrates, the easier they become to digest. Think about how a stalk of broccoli becomes softer when cooked. The danger, of course, is that you might cook vegetables and other carbohydrates for so long that the other essential nutrients get lost in the process. However, for cats, overcooked, mushy vegetables are better, as they are easier to digest.

For most of this book, "carbohydrates" will refer to grains and starchy vegetables, while "vegetables" will refer to other vegetables.

Fiber

Dietary fiber alleviates both diarrhea and constipation. It creates bulk in the stools because it has a water-containing capacity, and that bulk signals the body to maintain proper bowel function. It can also inhibit fat absorption and increase the excretion of cholesterol. Fiber binds with toxins and wastes and helps neutralize them before they do damage to the body. Fiber is a really significant component to any diet, but for cats it should be consumed in moderation. Cats typically do not need much fiber in their diet.

Fiber is found almost exclusively in plant foods: vegetables, fruit, legumes, whole grains, nuts, and seeds. There are two categories of fiber: insoluble (also called roughage) and soluble.

Insoluble fiber, such as cellulose, is found in the skins and stalks of fruits and vegetables, wheat bran, peanut shells, and cereals. It is not easily digestible. Too much insoluble fiber can irritate the gut lining.

Soluble fiber, such as fruit fiber (pectin, psyllium, and oat bran) binds with water. It is also divided into two groups: fermentable and non-fermentable fiber. Fermentable fiber, such as beet pulp, is used by the gut bacteria to promote healthy gut flora. Most cats would receive enough fibers in their natural diet from the gut or stomach contents of prey that they would consume.

Fats

Most of the time fat provides much of a cat's energy. Fats are a source of essential fatty acids and help make the food palatable.

Fat provides sustained energy to the body, and fat cells are the most efficient way that a cat's body stores energy for the future. Energy is measured in calories, and a gram of fat contains twice as many calories as a gram of either protein or carbohydrates.

Fats are essential to build and maintain arteries and nerves, as well as for energy production on the cellular level. It's also necessary for healthy kidney function and to keep your cat's skin and fur coat shiny and supple. Some vitamins are soluble (or digestible) only in fat; these include vitamins A, D, E, and K.

Fat comes in two varieties: saturated and unsaturated. Saturated fat comes from animal sources. Unsaturated fat is generally derived from nuts, seeds, and fish oils.

Essential fatty acids are a significant component of fats. These are not manufactured in the cat's body and are therefore considered essential nutrients to eat. You have probably heard or read about omega-3 fatty acids. Omega-3 is rare in common foods; it must come from sources such as fish or flaxseeds. Olive oil is a great source of omega-9 fatty acids.

Cold-pressed oils are considered the best sources of essential fats, and this is why flaxseed oil is located in the refrigerated section at the health food store. I would also recommend plenty animal fats in the cat's diet.

Micronutrients

Foods that must be eaten in small quantities are called micronutrients. Micro means "small." Micronutrients are vitamins and minerals. Some minerals are referred to as trace minerals because the body needs only the minutest quantities of these to function. Micronutrients are absolutely essential to sound nutrition in numerous ways. Not only do vitamins and minerals promote a cat's health and physical development, but they also regulate its metabolism and assist in the biochemical processes that release energy from digested food.

Vitamins

Today, numerous vitamins have been recognized and researched. It is likely that, through research and continued study, scientists will discover others. No vitamin acts alone. Together, and in conjunction with minerals, they perform in thousands of ways.

They have a major impact on digestion, metabolism, oxidation, reproduction, and growth. Fat-soluble vitamins include vitamins A, D, E, and K. These can be stored in the liver and fatty tissues. In high doses, they can be toxic. Water-soluble vitamins include vitamin C and the various vitamin Bs (thiamin, riboflavin, niacin, B6 [a.k.a. pyroxidine], folic acid, B12 (also called cyanocobalamin), pantothenic acid, pangamic acid, biotin, choline, and inositol). A cat must eat water-soluble vitamins every day because they are rapidly excreted in their urine and poop (a highly scientific term).

Whole Food Sources of Vitamins

VITAMIN A
Dairy: Cheese, milk, and yogurt. Eggs. Seafood: Crab, haddock, halibut, herring, lobster, mackerel, oysters, salmon, swordfish, brook trout, and lake whitefish. Meat: Organ meats. Grains: Cornmeal. Vegetables and Fruits: Asparagus, avocado, broccoli, carrots, green peas, leafy green vegetables, pumpkin, spinach, squash, sweet potato, and tomato, apples, apricots, bananas, blueberries, cherries, figs, grapes, mangos, nectarines, oranges, prunes, and tangerines.

VITAMIN B6
Vegetables and Fruits: Artichoke hearts and avocado, apples, apricots, bananas, dates, figs, mangos, plums, raisins, and strawberries.

VITAMIN B12
Dairy: Milk and yogurt. Fish: Tuna. Meat: Liver. Black strap molasses.

BIOTIN
Eggs. Seafood: Herring, oysters, and salmon. Grains: Soy flour, oats, whole wheat, and nutritional yeast. Vegetables and Fruits:

Cauliflower and lima beans. Meat: Organ meat. Nuts and Seeds: Almonds, peanuts, and walnuts.

VITAMIN C
Vegetables and Fruits: Guava, orange, papayas, and strawberries, alfalfa sprouts, asparagus, avocado, beets, bell pepper, broccoli, brussels sprouts, cabbage, cauliflower, green beans, green peas, leafy green vegetables, lima beans, potato, soybeans, spinach, squash, sweet potato, and tomato.

CHOLINE
Eggs. Grains: Wheat, soybeans, brown rice, and white rice.

VITAMIN D
Sunlight. Dairy: Swiss cheese, and milk. Eggs. Seafood: Cod liver oil, eel, herring, mackerel, salmon, sardines, and shrimp.

VITAMIN E
Eggs. Grains: Wheat germ. Vegetables and Fruits: Mangos, avocado, kale, and sweet potato. Nuts and Seeds: Almonds, hazelnuts, and sunflower seeds.

FOLIC ACID
Dairy: Milk, and yogurt. Eggs. Vegetables and Fruits: Apricots, dates, and oranges, artichoke hearts, and avocado.

INOSITOL
Egg yolk. Grains: Oats, and Wheat. Seafood: Herring, and oysters. Vegetables and Fruits: Apples, blackberries, cherries, dates, grapefruit, kiwi, oranges, nectarines, peaches, prunes, artichoke hearts, green beans, northern beans, lima beans, and navy beans. Meats: Beef liver, and chicken liver. Nuts and Seeds: Almonds, peanuts, and walnuts

VITAMIN K
Dairy: Milk, and yogurt. Oils: Soybean oil. Meats: Beef liver. Eggs. Vegetables and Fruits: Asparagus, broccoli, cabbage, cauliflower, green beans, peas, and chickpeas.

NIACIN
Seafood: Halibut, mackerel, salmon, shad, swordfish, and tuna. Grains: whole wheat, brown and white rice. Meats: Beef, lamb, pork, organ meats, chicken, and turkey.
Vegetables and Fruits: Dates, figs, guava, mangos, papayas, peaches, asparagus, avocado, mushrooms, green peas, potato, soybeans, and squash.

PANTOTHENIC ACID
Dairy: Milk and yogurt. Meats: Chicken, and turkey. Vegetables and Fruits: Apricots, bananas, dates, figs, guava, mangos, oranges, papayas, prunes, strawberries, and avocado.

RIBOFLAVIN
Dairy: Milk, and yogurt. Meats: Organ meats. Vegetables and Fruits: Apples, apricots, blueberries, boysenberries, dates, mangos, papayas, prunes, raisins, raspberries, strawberries, alfalfa sprouts, asparagus, avocado, broccoli, brussels sprouts, cauliflower, lima beans, mushrooms, green peas, rice, spinach, and squash.

THIAMINE
Dairy: Milk, and yogurt. Grains: Rice. Vegetables and Fruits: Bananas, blueberries, dates, figs, grapes, guava, mangos, oranges, papayas, prunes, raisins, asparagus, avocado, broccoli, cauliflower, green beans, leeks, lima beans, green peas, potato, soybeans, spinach, and sweet potato.

Rudy Edalati

Minerals

Minerals regulate diverse physiological and biochemical processes, including those pertaining to body fluids, nerve conduction, muscle contractions, and the structural integrity of the cell walls and membranes. When people refer to trace minerals, they are talking about those minerals the body requires in the minutest proportions. Trace minerals are essential elements of a good diet.

Minerals include calcium, chloride, chromium, copper, iodine, iron, magnesium, manganese, molybdenum, phosphorus, potassium, selenium, sulfur, and zinc. The list truly goes on and on. The best sources of minerals are vegetables, fruits, and legumes, although minerals are also found in other foods.

Whole-Food Sources of Minerals

CALCIUM
Bulgur wheat, cheese, cottage cheese, clams, mussels, oysters, salmon, carob flour, cornmeal, soy flour, figs, papayas, milk, yogurt, almonds, brazil nuts, broccoli, and leafy green vegetables.

CHROMIUM
Cheese, apples, clams, plums, prunes, chicken breast and skin, peanuts, thyme, and black pepper.

COPPER
Zucchini, pumpkin, chicken, turkey, pears, dates, figs, and apricots.

IODINE
Cheese, eggs, cod liver oil, cod, haddock, oysters, yogurt, kelp (seaweed), and table salt.

IRON
Oats, bulgur wheat, eggs, abalone, saltwater bass, striped mullet, saltwater mussels, oysters, sardines, scallops, weakfish, cornmeal,

16

rye, whole wheat, dates, figs, raisins, beef, lamb, beef and lamb liver, beef and lamb kidneys, chicken, turkey, chicken liver, avocado, Brussels sprouts, leafy green vegetables, butter beans, lima beans, kidney beans, lentils, green peas, pumpkin seeds, sesame seeds, white rice, soybeans, acorn squash, butternut squash, and Hubbard squash.

MAGNESIUM
Oats, cod, haddock, mackerel, striped mullet, oysters, shrimp, sole, cornmeal, rye, whole wheat, dates, figs, papayas, prunes, raisins, tamarinds, milk, yogurt, peanuts, sesame seeds, chicken, turkey, avocado, beets, leafy green vegetables, carrots, cauliflower, leeks, chickpeas, green peas, potato, pumpkin, brown rice, and spinach.

MANGANESE
Oats, blackberries, blueberries, boysenberries, dates, figs, grapes, pineapple, raisins, raspberries, strawberries, peanuts, and avocado.

MOLYBDENUM
Barley, buckwheat, beef kidney, lamb, lean pork, green beans, lentils, strawberries, yams, and tomato.

PHOSPHORUS
Barley, bulgur wheat, oats, cheese, cottage cheese, eggs, abalone, freshwater bass, bluefish, carp, clams, cod, crabs, freshwater crayfish, cusk, eel, sole, haddock, halibut, herring, ocean perch, oysters, red snapper, salmon, scallops, shrimp, smelt, swordfish, brook trout, tuna, cornmeal, rye, whole wheat, raisins, beef, lamb, organ meats, milk, yogurt, brazil nuts, cashews, peanuts, pumpkin seeds, sesame seeds, chicken, turkey, mushrooms, green peas, brown rice, butternut squash, and sweet potato.

POTASSIUM
Cottage cheese, saltwater bass, bonito, carp, clams, cod, haddock, halibut, Pacific and lake herring, striped mullet, mussels, oysters,

red snapper, salmon, sole, weakfish, buckwheat flour, cornmeal, soy flour, apples, apricots, bananas, dates, figs, guava, papayas, plums, prunes, raisins, tangelos, beef, lamb, organ meats, milk, yogurt, almonds, brazil nuts, cashews, peanuts, sesame seeds, chicken, turkey, artichoke, asparagus, avocado, beets, broccoli, cauliflower, leafy green vegetables, lima beans, mushrooms, green peas, bell pepper, potato, pumpkin, spinach, squash, sweet potato, and tomato.

SELENIUM
Tuna, bananas, barley, noodles, brown and white rice, beef, chicken, lamb liver, beef liver and kidneys, pork kidneys, cashew nuts, garlic, mushrooms, navy beans, and molasses.

ZINC
Cheese, cottage cheese, eggs, rye flour, dates, guava, papayas, raisins, most fruits have small amounts, milk, yogurt, peanuts, sesame seeds, chicken, and turkey.

Water

Water is as crucial for optimal health as any food. As mentioned previously, a cat should not consume too much water, but it is a necessary part of its daily nutritional consumption. If a cat is drinking water in excess, even when fed a proper home-cooked diet, there may be a physiological problem—whereby you should notify your vet immediately.

In any case, a cat should have access to fresh water at all times. Change the water in your cat's bowl every day. If you can provide spring water, that is ideal, for fresh water contains trace minerals. Filtered water is also good, although it contains no trace minerals; when you filter water to eliminate toxins, you also eliminate essential nutrients. Never use distilled water because it has been de-mineralized.

Watch out for a few water hazards. The first one is chlorine. Chlorine is nearly unavoidable these days in tap water, since it is added to the drinking supply at treatment plants in order to kill the microbes—bacteria, viruses, and parasites—that cause diseases. Chlorine is toxic, especially to the kidneys, liver, and heart, and it depletes the body of vitamin E and other essential nutrients. It is a strong oxidizing agent.

The second water hazard is lead. Lead comes from old pipes, so if you know you have these in your home, you must run the cold water for a couple of minutes to give the standing water in the pipes a chance to clear out. Then it should be drinkable. Never use hot tap water for drinking, as it strips lead from pipes. A third potential hazard is the nitrates in water that run off fertilized farmland and into the drinking supply in rural agricultural areas.

You must also keep in mind that if you have an indoor-outdoor cat, the water in the streams, creeks, and swamps they encounter can cause them stomach ailments if they drink from these supplies.

Open water may be stagnant and contain microbes and/or be polluted by chemicals. In my community in Maryland, the sewer system has a history of leaking into the surrounding waters because the pipes are old and rusty and have sprung holes. If your area has flooding or excessive rain, this may cause an overflow of your sewers as well. Do your best to be vigilant about water.

Heading to Hidden Deficits

Now that we have considered the nutrients that your cat needs and their whole-food sources, let us look at some of the hidden ways good nutrition may be sabotaged. Ideally, your cat will receive all the nutrients he or she needs from the meals you provide. However, there are several potential deficits that can rob your cat's food of its nutritional values. These may affect your beloved companion animal and its health even if you home cook and use whole-food ingredients.

Refinement

During food processing, nutrients in foods are taxed out. While you can replace vitamins and minerals synthetically, as processed cat food does with artificial ingredients, the choice is less than ideal. An example of a refined food that you may find yourself cooking with is white flour versus whole wheat flour. Whole wheat contains more fiber, vitamin K, phosphorus, and magnesium than enriched white flour. Try to use whole, fresh ingredients whenever possible.

Supplements

Believe it or not, over-supplementing can be just as bad, or worse, than under-supplementing your cat's food. This is because certain nutrients, such as fat-soluble vitamins, can and do become toxic in excess. Whereas water-soluble vitamins get flushed out of the body through the urine stream, fat can be stored in the liver and tissues, and fat-soluble vitamins get stored along with it.

Here are some general guidelines for supplementing, although they are certainly not set in stone.

Suggested Supplements for Cats

- ➢ L-carnitine—*helps weight loss*
- ➢ taurine
- ➢ vitamin E
- ➢ vitamin K
- ➢ B complex—*not stored in the body therefore must be given every day, especially for sick cats*
- ➢ Vitamin B12—coblamin: *In cats with long-term Gastrointestinal issues, Coblamin may be used to prevent deficiency.*

CHAPTER 3

Guidelines for Cooking for and Feeding Your Cat

The general rule of any cat's diet composition is that it should consist of 80 percent meat protein, 10 percent carbohydrates, and 10 percent vegetables. The recipes I cook at Barker's Grub are based on these ratios, unless there are health issues involved with the animal I'm cooking for. For instance, if a cat is sick or injured, I might increase the protein ratio. Cats will need more protein to combat their illness and aid in their recovery.

Unless obesity is an issue, do not restrict a cat's food intake. Feed all that your kitty will eat. A general feeding guideline is 2 cups of food, twice a day. The needs of individual cats may vary as much as 50 percent above or below this amount. Kittens and pregnant cats will need slightly more food in order to meet their increased nutritional needs. If in doubt about your cat's dietary requirements, always overfeed. Never, ever, limit your cat's food, as you can literally starve your animal. Also, ensure that your cat has ready access to clean fresh water each day.

Usually, feeding your cat twice a day is ideal. Once in the morning and once in the evening. Since your cat is receiving real home-cooked food, it is not a good idea to leave the food out for more than thirty-five minutes. As you know, real food will begin to

21

break down and spoil after that time. Remove what the cat has not consumed and either dispose of it or, if it's been in a cool area, put the rest back in the fridge.

An essential element in a cat's diet is fluid. When fed cooked food, you'll notice that your feline will tend to drink less water than if he or she was on a commercial diet. The home-cooked food you're preparing for them will hold a higher moisture content coming directly from the meat juices, or broth, and will have less sodium. The broth is one essential ingredient you should never throw away.

Warning: Despite popular belief, onions and garlic do not help control worms. In fact, onions can cause hemolytic anemia (such severe anemia that the hemoglobin bursts), which can result in death for the cat.

You can tell whether or not any reduction in your cat's appetite is from illness and not general aging if he or she exhibits the usual symptoms of an unhealthy animal, such as lethargy, a dull coat, and runny eyes. If in doubt, check with your veterinarian.

Malnourished cats: Cats that have been malnourished, such as strays or rescued cases of neglect, need 90 percent protein and higher overall calories.

Post-surgery cats: Cats that have been spayed or neutered, or are recovering from being hit by a car or other trauma, need higher protein, 90 percent, but not necessarily higher calories.

Cold weather conditions: If your cat regularly spends time outside in the wintertime, it will need more calories and a higher fat content to keep warm. Use fattier types of meat in your recipes.

If your cat is obese, you can change the ratios of what is in the food slightly and reduce the quantity at each serving. Remember, the ratio of protein should never fall below 80 percent as cats need the high protein proportion regardless of whether they are obese or not. Any reductions that occur in serving size should be moderate and over time. As I mentioned already, drastic weightless poses a huge shock to a cat's system with devastating consequences.

It is crucially important to rotate the protein in any cat's diet. It is important to note that every allergy that occurs in cats is *to* the protein. If your cat has a food allergy it is a great idea to rotate their food: the meat protein, the vegetables and the grain.

By rotating all of the food you may be able to control the food allergies. It is also important to note that if your cat is allergic to a specific food, by rotating the diet you can most likely avoid another allergy occurring.

Protein in the diet can come from chicken, chicken livers, chicken hearts and gizzards, lamb, beef, beef livers, eggs, and some fish like salmon or mackerel, as well as rabbit if you can find it. *(Warning: Rabbit is very high in parasites. If you're preparing to feed your cat this protein, be sure and always overcook the meat. It pays to be on the safe side!)*

The kind of meat protein that might work best for your cat is probably the one that's easiest for it to digest. Always pay special attention to your cat's eating habits. Observe how eager the cat is when you put the food down for it, or how your puss is able to tolerate the meat protein. If vomiting occurs after eating, see what foods have not been digested. This will make it clear to you that your cat may not easily digest these particular foods.

The reason that we or any animal including the cat, eat food is in order to get all the nutrients our bodies need to sustain and support healthy functions. We need to eat such a wide variety of foods so that we can receive all the nutrients offered in such a vast range of sources.

Warning: Do not reduce the amount of food your cat eats to make them lose weight. Remember, cats, unlike dogs, continue to use the same amount of energy regardless of their state of activity or their food intake. They need the same amount of calories whether they're sleeping or at rest or they're active and hunting.

Oftentimes, the color of foods, particularly fruits and vegetables, will indicate a particular nutrient it contains. For instance, the color of egg yolks has a lot to say about the hidden goodness within: the more red or orange the yolk, the higher the vitamin A content.

In order for your cat to maintain a full and healthy diet where all its nutritional needs are being met, remember to widen the variety of proteins, vegetables, and grains. This will definitely allow for a more complete and adequate diet.

There are no tricky preparations or confusing ingredients in a rotation diet. It simply includes changing the makeup of the food from week to week, over a month-long period. For instance, it is a good idea to do chicken one week, then rotate to another meat protein the next week, such as beef livers, or lamb. You can also get a little creative and to mix proteins, like eggs with liver, which go very well together.

It is also very important to mix and vary the vegetables included in your kitty's diet. Please, if you can, buy organic or local produce. Obviously we want our cats to have the freshest and "cleanest" produce possible, untouched by chemical processing or pesticides.

Also, it is great to buy vegetables seasonally, as nice "light" vegetables in the summer, such as squash and zucchini, do really well in the cat's diet. In fall and winter, sweet potato or pumpkin make wonderful additions to the cat's meal.

Outlined below is an example of the basic structure of the monthly rotation diet.

MONTHLY ROTATION DIET	
Week 1	Chicken
Week 2	Eggs & liver
Week 3	Beef
Week 4	Chicken hearts & gizzards

Obviously, depending on your inclination and/or budget, the form of the meat protein is up to you. Ground chicken is as good as chicken thighs or breasts. Boneless makes for easier preparation when the time comes to roll up your sleeves and get your hands dirty to blend your mixture. However, if stewing your meat, chicken thighs are best with their bones still in, as they add more flavor and nutrients to the dish from the stewing process.

The same can be said for beef. Whatever is easiest for you to prepare is going to be just fine for your puss to consume. Some cats may prefer a particular texture, but as I mentioned previously, if you're observing your cat's eating habits, you'll know what he or she responds to best.

Supplements

When it comes to supplementing your cat's food, it is probably easier and more convenient to buy already made supplements. You can add these to any meal that you will be preparing for your puss. Please consult your vet about particular brands that they would recommend.

You do not need to supplement your cat's diet every day. However, the exceptions to this are taurine, calcium, and oil. A cat's daily requirement for taurine is 80 milligrams. In chapter 11, I will provide you with the recipe for making your own calcium powder (calcium carbonate) from eggshells. If the fat content from the meat protein is plentiful in the food you are preparing, then it should be sufficient and you probably won't need to add extra oil.

Oils you can use for cats include fish oil (salmon, cod liver), flaxseed oil, and animal fats (butter, chicken fat, beef fat, lamb fat).

A suggested daily supplement routine might include

> ➢ 1 dash of salt or salt substitute
> ➢ 1 dash of calcium carbonate

> ➤ 80 mg of taurine
> ➤ 2 teaspoons of oil

A suggested weekly supplement routine may include:

Sunday	Monday	Tuesday	Wednesday
Multivitamin with oil	** Salt* ** Calcium* ** Taurine* ** Oil*	** Multi-vitamin with oil*	** Salt* ** Calcium* ** Taurine* ** Oil*

Thursday	Friday	Saturday
*Multivitamin with oil	** Salt* ** Calcium* ** Taurine* ** Oil*	** Salt* ** Calcium* ** Taurine* ** Oil*

Three-day supplementing with a multivitamin should be sufficient. If in doubt, always consult your vet. Also, if your cat suffers from kidney disease or urinary tract problems, consult your vet because some supplements can, in fact, exacerbate these problems.

Treats

Have you ever questioned what those creatively shaped little snack treats for your cat really consist of? Why is it that they have such a long shelf life? The fact is that, like dry cat food, these treats are full of preservatives. Even a few treats a day can add up to a significant amount of preservatives during the course of a cat's life. The safe thing to do is not overdose your kitty with treats, or anything else for that matter. Remember, everything in moderation!

Potential Food Source Dangers

Onions, whether fresh, cooked, dehydrated, or powdered, are problematic for cats. The oil in onions can affect the hemoglobin in the blood, resulting in symptoms such as anemia, rapid breathing, lethargy, vomiting, and even a possible heart murmur. If you suspect onion poisoning, contact your veterinarian immediately.

Sugar is not good for your pet, whether it's feline or otherwise. He or she does not require it at all nutritionally. For the most part, cats do not like sweet things naturally.

CHAPTER 4

Health Issues in Cats

At Veterinary Holistic Care in Bethesda, MD, Dr. Monique Maniet is convinced that most cat diseases are food related. She comments that dry cat food is simply not the appropriate food for these carnivores. She also comments that if the pet food industry knew exactly what the science of cat food is, then there would not be as many ailments that cats appear to have these days.

Dr. Maniet is convinced that the high carbohydrates and low bioavailability in the cat food is the culprit. She says that cats that consume dry food don't end up drinking enough water and thus concentrates the urine. This is a problem for cats with urinary tract ailments. The foods are highly processed at high temperatures. People are looking only for convenience.

Dr. Maniet suggests that nobody truly knows exactly what cats really need nutritionally. We're learning every day as we go along.

Gastrointestinal Problems in Cats

The rate of gastrointestinal problems in cats is very high. Many cats will develop problems of the gastrointestinal tract in their lifetime. Often the culprit is food allergies.

Dr. Maniet also comments about inflammatory bowel disease (IBD). She indicates that many cats that suffer from IBD for a very long time whose symptoms go untreated can develop cancer in the long run. IBD is the number one illness in cats that she sees in her practice. This condition is a major health issue for cats. Many cats with IBD, young and old, can also end up with pancreatitis and liver issues.

The second most common health issues seen by Dr. Maniet in her practice is hypothyroidism, directly linked to nutrition. She says that this problem could be due to the soy products added to commercial pet food. The next most common health issues that she sees are kidney problems and UTI problems.

Earlier, in chapter 3, we discussed the rotation diet. If your cat has gastrointestinal problems, you must rotate the diet all the time. This prevents new allergies from developing and controls any existing allergy issues that your cat may possess.

Please observe closely which foods your cat has a difficult time digesting. For instance, if you make a batch of food and not long after it finishes eating your cat throws it up, then you have a pretty good idea that there is a problem. Either the problem is allergy related or your cat simply cannot break down and digest that particular mix of food.

When feeding cats with gastrointestinal problems or disorders, start feeding only very small amounts of food at one time. Start by giving as little as a teaspoon.

Remember: when you give small meals, you must feed your cat at least six to eight times a day. Small amounts throughout the day will not overwhelm the cat's gastrointestinal tract. If your kitty responds well to the initial portions, continue to increase the amount of food while reducing the frequency of mealtimes.

Once your cat has transitioned to the new diet, remember to rotate it weekly to help control the allergies in your animal.

If your cat continues to vomit when offered the home-cooked food, and you have tried all of the recipes I suggest, please contact your veterinarian as soon as possible. Ensuring your cat is receiving adequate nutrients is paramount. Remember: cats can develop fatty liver disease and starve to death within a relatively short amount of time.

Vomiting, however, can also occur for your kitty regardless of specific allergy issues. Occasionally, cats will vomit and you may see some hairballs in it. Sometimes this problem can be relieved by adding a little extra oil to their food (fish oil or chicken fat is ideal). Of course, if excess vomiting is occurring, no matter what your cat is consuming, it is an urgent matter for your veterinarian's attention.

When vomiting and diarrhea are the result of your cat ingesting something toxic, what can often happen is that the cat's body becomes hypersensitive to everything it consumes for a while. You must be very careful about what you give it afterwards.

For gastrointestinal problems such as colitis, stomach ulcers, bacterial infections, and toxic poisoning, you can give your puss some un-pasteurized "live" culture yogurt. Even as soon as fifteen minutes after your kitty throws up you may want to offer it a teaspoon of yogurt. Yogurt coats the stomach and reintroduces natural flora, which aid in digestion, to the intestines.

When a feline has a particular disease, the diet should immediately be changed. Although it is not always the cause, or the cure, the diet must correlate and be designed to control the disease.

Kidney Disease

Make sure you cat is getting enough vitamin C in its diet to acidify the urine. However, if your cat has kidney disease of any kind, do not give it supplements. Because one of the jobs of the kidneys is to purify the body, when you supplement you're actually making the kidneys work harder.

Skin and Coat Problems

An animal's coat is one of the first places that illnesses present themselves. For example, thyroid conditions can cause thinning of the fur. Most problems with the skin and coat are related to a deficiency of omega-3 fatty acids. Supplementing your cat's diet with fish oil ensures it receives the essential fatty acids it needs as part of its daily diet. Time and time again I have seen this simple solution remedy the skin and/or coat concern.

Cancer

When a cat has cancer it needs an increased amount of calories in its diet. Cancer burns energy very quickly, and it is critical that the kitty does not lose lean muscle mass. Your cat will need frequent feedings of high protein and high fat food. Avoid carbohydrates such as rice or noodles and instead offer sweet potatoes, squash, and pumpkin. These carbohydrates have higher vitamin and mineral levels. Sweet potatoes are one of the more complete foods, rich in nutrients. Also, the more dark, leafy greens a cat eats, the better, due to their mineral content, especially iron.

Diabetes

The pancreas is a tiny organ that secretes insulin in the bloodstream to control blood sugar levels. It can produce too much or, in the case of diabetes, too little. Cats with diabetes must eat fewer calories, eat lower fat meals, and must have no refined sugars whatsoever. You must learn to keep your cat's diet incredibly steady so its insulin levels will be exactly maintained. This means feeding your cat the same thing, the same amount, at the exact same time every day.

Hyperthyroid and Hypothyroid Issues

If your vet has diagnosed this condition then your pet has an overactive thyroid gland. This means that the metabolism of your kitty is speeded up, and your puss is probably losing weight, despite dietary routines. Feeding it fish oil and fatty meats keeps its caloric intake high while it receives appropriate medical treatment.

The opposite condition is hypothyroidism, but cats never suffer from this condition.

Anemia

Anemia means there is too little iron in the blood and therefore not enough red blood cells being produced. This may occur as a product of surgery and also through an infestation of ticks or fleas. If you lift up your cat's lip and the gums look white, in addition to overall lethargy, you can probably assume your cat is anemic. To compensate nutritionally, you can feed your cat broccoli, spinach, liver, and eggs. All these foods are loaded with iron.

Gum Disease

Yes, cats get gum disease. If you catch a glimpse of your cat's teeth and gums when it yawns, you'll see pretty quickly if the gums are overly reddish in color, highlighted by yellowed, gunky teeth. Dr. Monique Maniet suggests that gum disease in a cat is an autoimmune response whereby its body reacts by starting to attack itself. Dr. Maniet believes that this response often begins as early as kittenhood and stays with the animal through its adult years. It is not uncommon for infections to develop, resulting in the need to remove teeth. A cat that has lost teeth will have trouble eating and maintaining weight and will feel pain. There is a secondary component to the implications of gum disease in a cat. If the bacteria in your cat's mouth gets so out of hand, then the gum disease can actually lead to infections of the kidneys, heart, and other organs, as it is transported through the bloodstream. A clean mouth is a pretty crucial part to your cat's overall good health!

Autoimmune Disorders

In recent years, it has become more common to acknowledge animals, including humans, having autoimmune disorders. I believe that these disorders are directly linked to allergies and other environmental stresses that persist in our current world. One of the most important roles that food and nutrients play is to build a healthy immune system.

Cats that are stressed or consuming a poor diet with too many carbohydrates and grains can develop a lackluster coat without shine or vigor. When cats do not receive adequate protein and there seems to be a lack of bioavailability, they will become fat and be in ill health.

Furthermore, at Barker's Grub, my dog and cat food catering company, we use only locally produced food sources. The meat, vegetables, and grains all come from the region where my cats and I reside.

I think this is an important element in working with your animal's allergies. The poultry and cattle need to graze on the wild vegetation that exists in your area, including our much-hated "weeds." This exposes them to the same environmental allergens that you yourself, and your animals, would be immersed in.

The benefits to this are that when your animal feeds on the locally produced food sources that you have cooked, their immune system will be stronger and allergies will be minimal.

I do not, however, believe in the benefit of global commerce when it comes to preparing food for my animals. There are now too many questionable practices in food preparation, on a national as well as an international scale, in order to feel comfortable offering it to my beloved companions. At least if it's local, you have some degree of access to knowledge about its production process.

Eating and buying locally is crucially important when cooking for your animal. Not only does it help the local economy, but most importantly it aids in the maintenance of your pet's optimum health.

Obesity

Most cats that are obese have become that way because they have had either no or very little exercise and a constant availability of food—most likely dry cat food left out at all times in order for the cat to "graze." The cat may possibly have even developed addictive eating habits out of boredom. These cats are at a high risk if developing diabetes.

By removing the accessibility of endless amounts of food and offering more adequate portioning, it is possible to give cats, like humans, the ability to lose weight. Also, another factor that may assist in weight loss for an obese cat is providing greater mental and physical stimulation.

A word of caution: a fat cat must not lose weight quickly or drastically. This may prove to be too great a shock to its system. Moderate weight loss over time is definitely a more reasonable expectation—for both the cat's health and for the long-term sustainability of the animal's appropriate weight.

If your cat cannot have access to the outdoors, and if you have the means, a cat room or cattery might be a good choice. This is definitely an investment for the long-term health of your cat.

I have a friend who actually enclosed her porch with screens and built little catwalks around the interior. It also had tree trunks and cat beds, toys hanging from the ceiling, and of course it revealed the stimulating, natural outdoor experience of the backyard. The cats could have the benefit of the fresh air without being at risk for getting hit by a car or hurt by other animals.

Other people I have known have built catwalks inside their homes. These are narrow, wall-mounted walkways where the cats can survey their territory from a favored raised perch. These may also include cat trees and other furniture, toys, and hideaways. In addition to the enhancement of the cats' lives, the homes seem so much more colorful and lively because of it.

When dealing with an obese cat, a change in the diet must occur so that the animal is being fed home-cooked food. This way you are able to control completely what the cat consumes.

Appropriate recipes for making these changes will be listed in chapter 11. Before giving a cat any weight loss recipe, please always start with the transition diet.

Most dry pet food has a lower fat content and a higher degree of fiber than "wet," or canned commercial cat food. This can increase the water excretion in the feces and decrease the water excretion in the cat's urine. This is a major problem because it increases the mineral content in urine, which causes urolithiasis.

In canned commercial cat food about 75 percent of the content is water, so it is, at least nutritionally, a better option to feed to your pet than dry food. What is even better, of course, is a natural home-cooked diet for your beloved puss.

Post-Surgery and General Stress

If your kitty has been recently spayed or neutered or undergone any other invasive surgical procedure, or if it's simply been experiencing general life stress, you may want to feed it food that is a little more gentle on the stomach, such as chicken and rice. Give the cat plenty of stewed meat protein. You can also mix a little bit of kelp powder into the food. These are high in vitamins and minerals, which will help in healing whatever ails your beloved puss. Make sure also that it receives cod liver oil every day.

Finicky Cats

Most veterinary medicine textbooks agree that finicky cats are made and not born. Ask any proud cat owner and they'll tell you just how very picky their beloved felines are! In contrast, cats are, by nature, wonderful eaters.

All cats need a rotation diet. They need a wide variety of proteins to fulfill their nutritional requirements. Some cats, however, will develop a fixed food preference. This is really important to avoid for different reasons. If, in the future, a health issue arises for your cat and its diet needs to be changed, it will be extremely difficult to do so if the cat's palate is not already exposed to different flavors and proteins. This can be avoided by mixing up the cat's diet right from the start. By introducing your cat to a variety of proteins, vegetables, and grains, you are training them not to be finicky eaters.

While the conditions I have mentioned above are not a complete list of every possible concern your cat may face, it does serve to illustrate that active role that nutrition plays in overall health, both preventive and restorative. It is critical that you speak with a veterinarian rather than attempt to simply treat your cat's ailments yourself. Veterinarians are trained to weigh all the factors that contribute to a given problem and, hopefully, keep themselves informed and updated on the most current medical research and findings.

First Aid and Emergency Care

If your cat has been poisoned, burned, electrically shocked, hit by a car, stepped on, or injured in some way and you suspect internal injuries or breakages, manage the trauma as best you can without making it worse and seek veterinary attention as soon as you safely can. Alternatively, if your cat is bleeding, choking, has inhaled smoke, or is having a seizure, do the same. The poor kitty may go into shock and require emergency medical treatment with intravenous fluids and adrenal steroids.

As a pet owner, you should have a reference guide for first aid for animals in your home. Here is a good one that I keep handy: *Pet First Aid* by Bobbie Mammato, DVM, MPH (Mosby Yearbook, 1997). This book is also co-sponsored by the American National Red Cross and the Humane Society of the United States.

Buy or create a good pet first aid kit. Supplies in this should include the following:

- rolled gauze
- gauze pads
- clean towels
- rectal thermometer
- antiseptic solution like Betadine or surgical scrub
- ice packs
- hydrogen peroxide (3%) for both treating open wounds and to induce vomiting.
- dry mustard
- baking soda
- milk of magnesia
- Pepto-Bismol for indigestion
- saline solution for rinsing eyes
- scissors
- Vet Wrap, a self-adhesive tape bandage

Small heating pads (from an outdoor supply or ski store) used to warm quickly in cases of shock.

Rudy Edalati

Holistic Pet Care: Complementary Medicine for Cats

Holistic veterinary medicine is an idea whose time is definitely now. In recent years, and with its celebration in media and television culture, America has rediscovered and accepted into the mainstream the principles of holistic health care and sound nutrition. This, of course, is as it primarily applies to human beings. However, it is also becoming a more popular choice for people to carry this practice over into the care of their animals.

You can find practitioners for this veterinary specialization now all over the country. In the Maryland community where I live, just outside Washington, DC, I work closely with two holistic vets who refer their clients to me on a regular basis for supplies of homemade cat food and nutritional consultations.

The first time I was ever really exposed to holistic veterinary medicine was when I was in my teens, and a holistic veterinarian names Joyce Harmon came to treat my horse, Haly. Dr. Harmon is now a contributing editor of *Whole Horse Journal*. My horse was a retired racehorse that kept rearing her head whenever I rode her. It was an involuntary jerk that would inevitably punch me in the face. The result, of course, was that I was riding in fear, and so was Haly, although it was clear that she was not doing it on purpose to hurt me.

Over a period of months, several veterinarians examined my horse and none were able to pinpoint or treat the problem. They prescribed anti-inflammatory drugs, but the symptoms persisted. Finally, another rider at the barn suggested I try working with the holistic veterinarian, even though many people at the barn thought the whole idea was a load of hogwash. I had no idea what to expect, but I figured it was worth a try.

When Dr. Harmon looked at Haley, she felt up and down the horse's spine with her fingers and discovered three vertebrae out of line. Over the course of six months, the vet came back three times and gave my horse chiropractic adjustments, realigning her spine, followed by acupuncture treatments. The acupuncture needles had small containers at their outer ends, which the doctor filled with B vitamins. The vitamins drained into Haly's body during the course of the sessions. When the injections were finished, the needles would pop out by themselves, about half an hour later. These injections made the horse relax its muscles and immediately stopped her head from thrashing back and forth.

To me this was fascinating work. I had never seen acupuncture performed on either human or animal. Haly calmly took to the hair-fine needles, rather than the expected panic and need for restraint. Dr. Harmon also showed me stretching exercises to do with Haly each day to promote her circulation. She showed me acupressure points for massage therapy. Afterwards, the change in my horse was remarkable. Haly felt better, so she became much more willing overall, and we both consequently enjoyed our rides together. No more fear (from either of us), no more discomfort.

Since that experience I have also seen and heard numerous cases of dogs and cats that have been treated successfully through non-traditional therapies. Cats respond to acupuncture, chiropractic care, and homeopathy just as well as larger animals do. Combined with sound nutritional principles, holistic veterinary care is amazingly effective, but you have to be willing to work with the veterinarian and be patient. Their therapy is not a miracle cure; it is a process that uses progressive treatments to maximize its full benefits. Holistic medicine does not attempt to cure isolated symptoms; rather, it is centered on bringing the whole body into a balanced state of optimal wellbeing. As we ourselves know, this is a lifelong enterprise.

Having witnessed the remarkable results of holistic veterinary medicine firsthand, I am now a strong proponent of these non-conventional methods. Holistic practitioners are highly educated healers, who first earn their degrees as mainstream veterinarians and then continue with additional training. This "complementary" medicine works well in combination with western drugs and surgical procedures. It is often preferable to traditional treatments for non-invasive and non-traumatic procedures that are often the first method of treatment.

Most holistic vets study homeopathy and Chinese herbal remedies, and some are trained in acupuncture and chiropractic care. Holistic veterinarians are also trained to understand and take into consideration the emotional component of treatment and healing. The holistic veterinarians with whom I have spoken uniformly believe that proper wholesome nutrition is essential to promote and maintain optimum health.

When a holistic veterinarian is working to diagnose a cat's condition, in addition to the physical and behavioral symptoms that may indicate an underlying problem, he or she takes into account the cat's genetic background, vaccination history, and dietary regimen. Because the cat's genetic makeup obviously cannot be changed, the holistic vet will assess the vaccination protocols and modify its diet.

The animal will be placed on a homemade diet, with food and supplements formulated to deal with its specific diagnosed condition, such as kidney disease, allergies, arthritis, and congestive heart failure. Additionally, the vet may also prescribe homeopathic remedies, chiropractic sessions, or acupuncture sessions to alleviate symptoms, and even drugs and surgery when necessary.

Herbs

Plants are the basis for many of our conventional modern drugs, even the synthetic ones. Herbal medicine is the oldest form of medicine in the world. The World Health Organization states that 74 percent of plant-derived medicines have modern counterparts whose healing purposes correlate with the traditional and sometimes ancient uses of these herbs.

The difference between a pill that a mainstream veterinarian would prescribe and an herb that a holistic veterinarian would prescribe is that the pill likely contains an isolated active ingredient, whereas herbs are whole plants. Whole plants are more balanced. Drugs address symptoms, whereby plants, even fruits and vegetables, often have tonic effects on the body that drugs do not. Instead, they strengthen the entire immune response.

Holistic veterinarians understand the nature of herbs and how to determine the proper dosage of an herb for your cat's condition by weight and symptom. These can be given in capsule form or sprinkled dry onto food. Usually cats are not readily accepting of pills by mouth, so the dry form over the food is a much better option. Sometimes the vet may even give you a bottle of tincture, an herb extract in an alcohol base.

Acupuncture

In addition to herbs, acupuncture is the primary tool of traditional Chinese medicine. Acupuncture works on all kinds of species and sizes of animal, including humans. If a cat has localized pain or stress, acupuncture can be very effective. Along with treating symptoms of pain, it is also used for every condition and disease the body sustains. Acupuncture can treat a wide variety of conditions: asthma, ulcers, arthritis, colitis, diabetes, back pain, eczema, even deafness. It is known to stimulate endorphins, the brain chemicals that induce euphoria and pain control.

In the United States, veterinarians who choose to practice this specialty are members of the American Association of Veterinary Acupuncture. See the resources section at the back of this book for help in locating a practitioner.

Homeopathy

Homeopathy is based on the principle that "like cures like." After examining the cat's symptoms, the homeopathic veterinarian would prescribe a remedy that, given to a healthy cat in high doses, would produce the same set of symptoms. This is done in order to catalyze the cat's own immune response. The remedies are extremely diluted substances, such as herbs, minerals, and other natural materials, so they will not poison your puss. When the remedy works, it has no side effects. When it doesn't work, there is no harm done to the cat. This kind of treatment is better for non-life threatening conditions, as it can take a while for the body to respond.

The government doesn't yet license or recognize homeopathic veterinarians; it is a voluntary designation. However, you can locate a practitioner in your area by contacting the Academy of Veterinary Homeopathy. See the resource section at the end of this book.

CHAPTER 5

Neurotic Cats and Neurotic Cat Owners

It appears that neurotic cats have become increasingly abundant. In the next chapter, I will discuss my own problem cat, Princess Pooty, and what she was telling me about her neuroses. Aside from my own observations and experiences with my own kitties, I also have many clients with cats that possess neurotic disorders.

If your cat is not engaged in a stimulating and active environment, boredom and an overactive mind may take over. Both a cat's body and its mind must be exercised. Cats are hunters. They must exercise their hunting instincts and abilities. By doing so, they will be maintaining the level of activity similar to that which they would find in their natural environment. Thus, they will not begin to get fat and develop obesity issues (unless food is made available to them constantly).

So many cats lounge about their house bored and immersed in an overachiever lifestyle. The cat has been so overindulged that their human companions have essentially made them useless. This absolute redundancy of the cat's natural abilities is when boredom sets in and neuroses develop.

The only answer to a neurosis is stimulation. My cat Pooty, who, as I mentioned previously, had her own degree of neuroses, made a point to show that she wanted to engage her "hunting" instincts.

She liked to pretend to "kill" tissues—used tissues, or put more simply, my old snot-rags. She would either find one from in the trash or pick one that hadn't quite made its way there yet. She would often pretend that this was a mouse that she had trapped and was happily torturing to its death. Then she would bring it and drop it at my feet—a token of her loyalty and bragging rights for her prowess as a masterful huntress. I would show her how impressed and proud I was of her and praise her with a pat and a scratch and a "what a good girl!" I could just see how proud of herself she was.

This is a wonderful example of a cat creating its own stimulation, with its human companion offering positive reinforcement to encourage the behavior.

Many of my cat-owner clients complain to me of their felines demonstrating neurotic behaviors. In some instances they even go as far as medicating their beloved puss with drugs in order to try and alleviate the compulsive behaviors. Sometimes the simplest of solutions would be just to create some kind of stimulation for the cat.

As I have just discussed, neurotic cats are a problem. However, in my opinion, neurotic cat owners are even worse. Often a cat may have developed physical or behavioral problems because of its owner. The owners themselves may be the source of the issue, even the reason that the cat has developed the neuroses or become ill in the first place.

Nobody is perfect and everyone these days seems to have his or her own slew of issues. However, some people project their own problems or negative energy on the animals in their care. These may be either mental or physical issues, and sometimes both. I have had, on numerous occasions, clients who suffered physiological problems and projected them onto their cats. From my outside perspective this was obvious, but for those inside of the problem, it is not always that easy to see.

Obsessive disorders have also appeared to become more prominent in current society, or perhaps they're now just more openly spoken about. These too can affect a pet that is constantly immersed in this kind of environment. A person may have an issue with a particular food, and they may, in turn, say that their cat has the same issue. An example of this may be liver. Perhaps it's easier to make the blanket statement that "we" don't like liver, when it really means "I."

I cannot speak for how to treat people in order for them to overcome their issues and neuroses. I believe that if help is sought to address neurotic and obsessive behaviors and a person is in a healthy state of mind and body, their respective animals will respond to this healthy projection in kind.

In some unfortunate instances, however, people are never aware of their own compulsions and in turn don't see how they are affecting their animals in a negative way.

Always remember: a healthy cat is a happy cat, both physically and behaviorally. There have been many instances that I have tried to pick up or hold an overweight cat, or observed someone else trying to do so, and the situation turns ugly for everyone. The poor cat screams, or tries to scratch and bite.

Clearly the cat is not comfortable. They may even be in a degree of pain. I think we would be too, of someone had tried to pick us up while heavily overweight and suffering from the health issues that obesity causes.

Cats are hunters. They must exercise their minds as well as their bodies. In order to have a healthy cat the food and the environment must be stimulating. A cattery, an enclosed porch, cat trees, space with lots of cat toys, a room with a view, fresh air and live surround sound (open windows with screens in place do the trick), and access to plenty of catnip are all crucially important.

If you can also take your cat outside, you'd really have him or her in raptures of excitement. As unusual as it might sound, leashes are not just for dogs! You can put a harness on your cat, add the leash, and head out into the yard. Always remember, a cat needs a harness if you leash it—relying on just the collar spells trouble, especially for animals that are renowned escape artists and contortionists. Also, please use common sense and don't assume that if they are leashed, the cat is fine to be left outside without you. Cats can panic and strangle themselves getting wrapped up in the leash.

The joy of taking your cat outside is that you get to experience the pleasure with them. It doesn't need to be for long, perhaps a few minutes—the longer the better, of course. Your cat will be so appreciative and simply overjoyed at the access, no matter how small, to its natural environment.

Another thing to be aware of in a physical sense is your household safety. Not something you'd typically think of in terms of a pet's health, but remember: what's good for you is not always good for your animals.

Some household plants can be poisonous to cats. You can probably ask your vet to be more specific about this, but cats in general like to nibble on plants. The best plant you can provide for your cat is catnip. What's even better is if it is freshly grown in pots in your home. It can be an additional beautiful and aromatic herb for your household, as well as providing the cat with something to "graze" on that it really loves.

Ultimately, your cat's health is dependent on you, their human companion. Remember: regular, nutritious feeding, fresh water, and physical and mental stimulation are all key elements in ensuring the optimum health and happiness of your beloved cat.

CHAPTER 6

Implications for a Bored Cat

Companionship for a cat is vital. Some cat owners may say that their cats really don't like other cats. We've all seen the cat with the bad attitude, not afraid to show it to any other cat encroaching on its territory.

Is this really an accurate assumption to make, that the cat is happier on its own? Its owners may very well be saying that simply because they don't want to have a companion for their own feline. Maybe that's just too much work. Maybe that's just another round of vet bills. Maybe that's just another mouth to feed and more litter to clean up.

If a cat owner heads off to work for at least an eight-hour day, and in many cases so much longer, can you imagine how lonely their poor cat must be?

It has been suggested that cats prefer a more solitary lifestyle, that they're more than happy to be the top cat—the only cat—in the house. That seems crazy to me: to have the company of another being like yourself, to play, share and bond with, is not a basic need for cats? Is companionship not an important element in the positive health and wellbeing of a pet, domesticated for its own companionship tendencies? Even the domesticated feline's big cat cousins move in family groups in the wild and are extremely bonded to each other.

Allow your beloved pet the joy of company from another cat. Even the most rigid, functionally fixed cat will come around in time. They will slowly begin to appreciate the company of another cat.

Socializing cats as early as possible is essential. Exposing them to other cats when they are kittens will prove to be much more beneficial for the cat in the long run.

Also, if you have a kitten, handling it as much as possible from early on will make it a more confident and affectionate cat. Even as a kitten, a cat's personality is apparent. If it is relatively shy and skittish, give it as many opportunities as possible to be around you— even if you are not directly giving it attention. Becoming familiar with your tone, your presence and your movements will enable the cat to develop a sense of trust and confidence around you.

Obsessive Compulsive Behaviors

Obsessive compulsive behavior in cats is not uncommon. As I mentioned previously, my beloved cat Pooty had this disorder.

When I first found Pooty all those years ago, she was in the gutter and she looked terrible. Her entire backside was bald. I thought this sweet girl must have been abandoned and abused— thrown out like a piece of trash. Poor little Pooty, scavenging in the dumpster for scraps.

It wasn't until much later, after I'd had her for around three weeks, that I noticed that she was plucking chunks of fur out of her back end with her mouth. I saw her tearing out her fur with such fervor that it scared me. I wondered if she had some kind of skin disease. Fleas, maybe? The vet treated her for all the possible conditions that may have been affecting her patchy state. However, months went by, and she was still going at it, yanking at tearing at herself, literally pulling her hair out.

Then, I also noticed her engaging in other odd, repetitive behaviors. She began to repetitively lick one spot on the wall. She focused on a spot and proceeded to go at for hours, lick after lick. Around the house, there would be obvious areas of her "affection," with the paint or wall surface covering faded or licked away from the pressure of the regular and repeated licking. This annoying habit, which offered a wet, slurpy, clicking sound, would literally occupy Pooty for hours at a time. Pooty was not partial to a certain time of the day either. Often, in the middle of the night, I would hear the incessant sound begin and settle in for a sleep-interrupted night.

This latter habit really cemented for me that Pooty suffered from obsessive compulsive behaviors. Either that or she'd become addicted to the lead in the wall paint!

The only real cure for Princess Pooty was to create stimulation for her. We tried toys and cat trees, but they were simply not enough. I finally had to make the decision to let her go outdoors, in the hope that this natural stimulation would be what Pooty craved in her hours of repeated hyper-focus on the wall.

It was not an easy decision for me. I, like so many other caring and cautious cat owners, was concerned about the dangers that lurked in the vast openness of the outdoors for Pooty. So many possible things might happen, like getting hit by a car or being attacked by a dog or other wild animal or simply getting herself stuck someplace in her curious explorations.

Despite my reservations, I made the decision to let her venture out. I did not live on a busy street, and I had a relatively long driveway, so these factors eased my fears a little.

As soon as Pooty could go into the garden, she simply stopped her obsessive compulsions. I know that may sound miraculous at the very least, but it's true. With regular field trips into her "wild habitat" (our rather boring and nondescript backyard), Pooty stopped plucking at her fur. She stopped her licking frenzies on the walls. She simply stopped demonstrating a need to channel her pent up energy on anything but her outdoor fun zone. And fun did she have! Gone were her mighty attempts at hunting tissues. She now had the real, live prey to go after instead—which she showed evidence of, regularly.

Upon reflection, I suppose Pooty's weird behaviors were probably why her original owners abandoned her in the first place all those years ago. What a revelation, both for me as well as her, to find such a simple thing could make such a difference to the quality of her life. You really cannot deny that an animal's natural instinctive imprint is really not something to stray too far from in the domestic setting.

Pooty seems so much happier to smell the air around her, watch the flowers change with the seasons, gaze upon the many birds she dreams of catching, and graze now and then on some nice, fresh grass.

CHAPTER 7

Purebred Cats and the
Reality of Inbreeding

Cats that are inbred appear to have a multitude of illnesses, as I have witnessed with so many of my cat clients. A good amount of my clients have "fancy" cat breeds with official sounding names and distinctive physical features, bred for those exact attributes. However, these cats also appear to have so many physical and health issues that they really should not have been bred at all.

The poor cat suffers so badly for the vanity of their owner, who desires features that particular people find amusing or attractive. People give so little thought to the actual genetics and overall health of the animal that they are breeding. Inbreeding, or line breeding as it is sometimes called, can contribute to numerous ailments, such as breathing problems in some Persian cats and overall ill health.

Why would anyone believe that it is okay to breed an animal to their siblings, parents, aunts, or uncles? This is clearly not an accepted practice that anyone would tolerate, yet alone promote, in our own species. Just think about the genetic implications of breeding to your own bloodline and gene pool.

So why has it become accepted and celebrated as a natural practice for a "pure" pet? In my humble opinion, however beautiful or exotic the cat may be—and to me all cats are beautiful—the best kitties are created through natural selection. Mix up the gene pool and throw it as far from each cat's existing line as possible, I say! Like stray cats you can find all over the world. The true beauty is seeing how technicolor and different all cats can be.

Interestingly, it appears that many feral cats do not succumb to the many illnesses that the domestic cat falls prey to, for exactly these reasons. They are in control of their own natural diet and possess such a strong immune system because they have to be in the best possible shape to survive in the wild. Even our domestic shorthaired cats (the "mutts" of the cat world) do not have as strong an immune system as these feral cats. Surely we should pay attention to that little detail from nature.

Magic and Miles

One of my clients had two beautiful seal-point Siamese cats. They were brothers, Magic and Miles. These two adorable cats were in and out of the veterinarian's office constantly. They both suffered terribly from skin and food allergies.

On a daily basis, at least once a day, they both would vomit. Each cat also had a very bad under-bite and a bad case of the gum disease gingivitis. Since they had these last two issues, their food had to be pureed.

Magic and Miles could only stomach either beef and barley, or chicken and rolled oats. Through this somewhat bland diet, we were able to control some of the problems they had. In my opinion, the health issues or side effects that these beautiful boys had to suffer through was the direct result of their inbreeding.

Clementine the Streetwalker and her Kittens

Clementine is a sweet, amazingly affectionate, petite, medium-long-haired gray and white kitty. I first found this lovely sweet girl on the side of my own country road in the dead of night. I was driving home late from running some errands when my headlights came across some shadows of life in the darkness. Initially, I spotted two of her kittens trying to get across the road, like two teeny white fluffy balls. Thank goodness I was driving slowly, maybe 20 miles an hour (the only way to drive in rural areas if you want to play it safe for both you and the local wildlife). I stopped at once and decided I needed to see what exactly had just come across my path.

I got out of the car and realized that they were, in fact, tiny kitties, maybe a few weeks old. I managed to grab them both and ran back to my car. As a regular animal rescuer, I had a cat carrier box in the car that I was able to put them inside. I went back outside and looked into the woods, trying to see if I could spot any other babies. I heard something like a meow, so I grabbed my flashlight from the car and started in the direction of the noise.

I could see a scraggly-looking cat and some more kittens with her. I called out to her in my own version of a meow. She came toward me, ever so cautiously. For all she knew, I had taken two of her babies and maybe I would be a source of danger to her and the remainder of her litter.

I kept up with the meowing noises and soon I was petting her. Being the sweetheart that she is, she began to purr, and with her in my arms the rest of her babies came running. I grabbed these four kittens and added them to the box, as well as their sweet momma. I cannot tell you the relief I felt taking these lost kitties back to my farm, only minutes away from that very spot, just a little farther down the road. I knew I had just made a difference in helping these babies' chances for survival.

Clementine, as she was later named, was in such poor condition. Her fur was matted and scraggly, with patches missing. She was so skinny, which was frighteningly obvious, despite being a medium-long-haired cat. She had, of course, been nursing her babies, which put added nutritional stress on her own already small body.

I had them all checked out first thing the next day by my veterinarian, and despite their physical appearances, they were all pronounced healthy (with the exception of the runt baby, Sophie, who had an upper-respiratory infection resulting in gunky eyes and needed eye drops). I started feeding Clementine chicken and rice as often as she would eat it throughout the day. As her kittens were still nursing, she needed as much nutrition as she could possibly get.

Within days, you could see a dramatic difference in her appearance. Her fur became more fluffy and healthy looking, and she began to put on weight. Her kittens also started to gain weight and were able to fight off any upper-respiratory infections they had. Their eyes cleared up and became bright, and their coats were shiny and clean.

Clementine and two of her kittens, Sophie and Tabitha, were adopted by my brother's family. They now live in a clean, caring house, where they are fed wholesome home-cooked food. They constantly keep the three dogs on their toes (and in their place!) and dream of one day catching the caged gerbils they "hunt" in the living room.

This is a far cry from her streetwalker roots, but it's a change I know Clementine must be thankful for. Although she never ventures outside, she is happily stimulated in her safe new home. To look at her now—you would never believe this is the same cat that had the scraggly fur and skin-and-bones appearance. She looks happy and healthy and at least ten years younger!

CHAPTER 8

To Vaccinate or not to Vaccinate

W hen I adopted my first kitten, I decided to name her Ashley—Kat Ashley to be exact. Like all newly adopted kitties, she had just received her first round of shots. Like any new cat owner, I was excited and overjoyed at bringing home the newest addition to the family.

However, that picture perfect little homecoming was rather short lived. When I took her home, later that night, she appeared to be convulsing, and a flow of foam was leaking out of her mouth. I was horrified. I had no idea what on earth was happening to Ashley or why. I didn't know what to do for her, and I was worried that there was something seriously wrong.

Within minutes the episode was over, and she began to walk and play around. Just like that, like nothing had happened. Luckily for Ashley, she demonstrated a quick recovery from that particular episode. Unluckily for me, I worried about what it meant and whether it would happen again. Just as I feared, the next day it happened again.

Thousands of dollars and many vets later, no one had any idea what was even remotely wrong with her. One vet suggested we try a spinal tap. Another vet said her walk was a little weird and that she was extremely ill—at death's door!—and maybe I wanted to consider euthanizing her. Ashley, instead, was put on a course of Phenobarbital.

Not one vet even had the remotest idea why she suffered convulsions at the age of eight weeks.

The vet technician who had vaccinated her by the base of her neck had no idea either. My questions continued: could the vaccine have caused an inflammation of the brain stem or spine? The vet consensus was "We don't know." Poor Kat Ashley was on so much Phenobarbital that she did not even exist in this realm of consciousness.

Soon after, at the age of ten weeks, she went into heat. Ten weeks! Just a baby herself. I questioned why she was going into heat so early and again pondered on the connection between the medication and this possible side effect. Yet again, none of the vet experts knew a thing.

The one veterinarian who'd indicated to me that euthanasia was my best option said that Ashley had very little time to live. With a comment like that ringing in my ears, I decided to take her off the Phenobarbital completely. I reasoned that if she was going to die anyway, then at least let her be conscious and engaged in her surroundings, not in some overmedicated, drug-induced, comatose state.

Slowly we reduced the dosage of her medication—first by a quarter, then by a half—until she was weaned off it completely. Meanwhile we had decided to put her on a completely home-cooked diet consisting of liver and a variety of different proteins. As the transition took place, amazingly, she never had a seizure. We monitored her responses really carefully, and we were so relieved to see the seizures cease. To this day, twelve and a half years later, Kat Ashley, although somewhat slow and a little different from other cats, is thriving.

I believe she is a little different from other cats due to the high amounts of Phenobarbital she was given at such an early age by the vets.

Vaccines are, of course, a necessity. But, when given in excess, vaccines can prove more harmful to the animal's body and can cause immune system issues. When it comes to Ashley, we still vaccinate her for rabies, but we do not vaccinate her for anything else.

Over-vaccination in cats that are old, feeble, sick, or injured can actually be counterproductive. An already stressed immune system can be pushed to its limits, and sometimes over the edge, by over-vaccinating.

There is a test called a Titer that can be given to cats. This measures the immunity level of the vaccine in a cat's blood. I would always get this test done for cats that I believe should not be vaccinated. For indoor cats or cats who never venture outside, Titers are the best form of control.

Rabies is the one vaccination that is nonnegotiable for cats. It absolutely must be administered for all cats, even those who don't get to go outside.

Dr. Maniet states that over-vaccinating is a serious problem for cats, especially the multi-vaccinations (combos), as they can trigger allergies and autoimmune problems. She says that it is a better idea to do a Titer. She says that it is the sole responsibility of the veterinarian *not* to vaccinate an unhealthy animal. Vets should be responsible in making sure they are not sending an animal's immune system into a downward spiral. If a cat has been vaccinated in the past, you can do a Titer to measure the immunity levels for specific medical threats.

She also says that only a small percentage of cats exposed to feline leukemia actually ever get sick, provided that the cat has a strong immune system, often reinforced through quality wholesome nutrition.

CHAPTER 9

Feeding and Cooking Methods—Raw Feeding

In my opinion, raw feeding is very questionable. I certainly don't advocate it, and you will not find any of my recipes that include any kind of raw ingredients as the final product.

One issue I have with raw feeding is that there is always a risk of your cat contracting salmonella. This bacteria does not get the chance to be cooked off through the cooking process. It can cause terrible gastrointestinal symptoms and can pose significant danger to any animal.

Another problem that occurs with a raw food diet is the potential for bones being still within the meat. Even the tiniest fragments can do serious damage. Risks include choking and perforation of the abdomen.

Raw vegetables are also a no-no in my book. Cats simply cannot break them down digestively. In order for your cat to be able to break them down and thus to receive the nutrients from them, the vegetables need to be well cooked, even mushy. Remember, cats cannot convert beta-carotene to vitamin A. Vegetables full of beta-carotene, like carrots, need to be well cooked in order for that to happen.

I don't believe that there has been enough scientific research and proof completed to truly stand behind raw food as a safe and quality diet for cats, or dogs for that matter. I do believe in the one thing we all (hope we) intrinsically possess—common sense.

First of all, it is important to understand what happens to meat at different temperatures. This really helps justify the rationale for why you would, or would not, feed it to an animal for optimum nutritional value.

When meat is stewed, cooked at moderate temperatures for a longer time, and not pressure cooked at higher temperatures, the amino acid availability is increased. This means that upon ingestion, you would receive more from the protein than you would when the amino acid availability had been lost through overcooking, or through the exposure to a far higher heat.

Also, new data indicates that quality nutrients are not lost when meat is stewed, as opposed to some other cooking methods. The juices from the meat are also important to keep in the cooking process. Essentially, by not getting rid of the juices, you have helped to concentrate the nutrients that these contain in combination with the meat itself.

How to Cook for Your Cat

Your kitchen is a place where you can bond with your cat. At times people may feel intimidated or anxious about beginning the process of cooking for their feline, but I am here to reassure you that it is a very simple task—like whipping up some eggs for yourself or throwing together a quick meal for your family.

Begin by cooking small amounts for your cat. Remember, the proportions of home-cooked food will be small as you transition from commercial pet food. You might even invite friends over and get together to begin your new healthy cooking method as a group: a Kitty Grub cooking party! Maybe while you're working together, you can chitchat over some wine and catch up with your human companions. You might even like to make it a weekly or monthly event, where you rotate to each other's homes in order to prepare your puss' favorite dinners.

If you prefer to work alone with simply the company of your curious cat, then the chance to unwind with some music and a glass of wine is a lovely way to spend an hour or so of your day.

It is important to begin by taking baby steps, trying smaller amounts of each recipe. Pick a simple recipe to start with and as time goes by you'll be making all the recipes by memory and even creating some of your own!

Preparing to Cook

You need very little specific equipment to cook the Kitty Grub meals. Since we are cooking fresh whole foods, most of the prep work lies in chopping vegetables and meats into manageable pieces in order to cook. In addition, you will need utensils, mixing bowls, and cooking pots—all items you probably have and use regularly in all your cooking preparations. Other than that, all you need is enough containers to hold the food you've made in your fridge or freezer for the week. Here's a more complete list:

- 2 sharp chopping knives, one for meat and one for vegetables.
- A chopping board. I use a wooden one that goes easily into the dishwasher.
- A colander, to drain your vegetables.
- A food processor, if you prefer to chop larger amounts of produce in this way.
- A small electric coffee grinder for powdering herbs and supplements.
- 2 really large pots that will each hold up to 2 gallons of liquid (these are for the weekly batches).

- 2 pots that will hold 8 cups of liquid (these are for the single-serving recipes).
- 1 slotted spoon.
- 1 pasta ladle.
- 1 spaghetti spoon.
- 1 ice cream scoop.
- 1 skillet, 12 inches in diameter and with a 2-inch rim.
- 2 large mixing bowls that will each hold up to 2 ½ gallons of liquid. I prefer metal, as they are lighter and easier to clean (these are for the weekly recipe variations).
- 2 small mixing bowls that will each hold up to 1 gallon of liquid. (These are for single-serving recipes).
- 2 or 3 wooden spoons.
- Room in your fridge or freezer to hold your cat's meals for the week ahead.
- Numerous plastic Tupperware-style containers or Ziploc bags for single servings—something that will fit 2–3 cups of food. Rubbermaid makes a 2.2-gallon square or rectangular container (which I like) that can hold the cat's food for the whole week.

Shopping for Ingredients

In my business of wholesome pet nutrition, I have learned a few things that will make your life as a Kitty Grub chef a little simpler.

Protein: All Kitty Grub recipes are built around the source of primary protein(s). For the most part, the core ingredients are interchangeable from meal to meal; however, I rarely substitute veal, pork, or tuna. I don't use veal because of the way the animals are treated. I worry that tuna may pick up heavy metals such as mercury. Fresh fish contains whatever has gone into the water, which contains increasingly high amounts of pollutants and waste products. The canned variety of tuna, on the other hand, just isn't as good as fresh.

Obviously it is crucial to cook meats really well in order to prevent certain microbes from being passed on. Chicken may carry salmonella, for example, and pork can carry *Trichinella spiralis*, which can cause trichinosis. Toxoplasmosis is a microscopic parasite that can contaminate beef and lamb and cause illness in humans, even affecting developing fetuses. So it is essential to take sanitary precautions when preparing these meats for your cat.

When handling food products, thoroughly wash the cutting boards, surfaces, and utensils, and scrub your hands and fingernails. A usual symptom might be a mild case of diarrhea. This is not life threatening, as are salmonella and trichinosis. Unless the immune system is compromised, the body fights it off. Most of these food-borne pathogens may be mistaken for a mild bout of the flu. If your cat is sick—in any way—do not give it raw meat.

Here is a list of proteins commonly found in my recipes:

- beef
- chicken (including hearts, livers, and gizzards)
- eggs
- fish: salmon, mackerel, tilapia, etc.
- lamb
- turkey
- cottage cheese

You can use any cuts of meat for my recipes. Remember, cooking at home can, and should, be economical.

You should also keep in mind to ask your local butcher for "free-range" farm meats. This ensures that you get the highest quality. Free range means not only that the chicken is being given organic feed and the chance to roam in a huge pen, but the pen is also clean, well maintained, and shared by only a few other chickens. The definition of organic and free range may differ from food product to food product, because currently these terms are not regulated. However, it is still a better bet that any other labeled meat. If you have a local farm that purports to keep their animals free range, it may require a little investigation to verify their practices.

Produce and supplements: Take the time to familiarize yourself with your local health food store and farmer's market, if you are not already a regular customer. These are usually the best sources of high quality vegetables and nutritional supplements in any community.

In order to really ensure that you're giving your cat the best in food quality, I advocate cooking with organically grown produce to avoid pesticides and other chemicals. If organic foods are exorbitantly priced in your area—although actually they've become more reasonably priced and readily available in recent years as demand has grown—then your alternative is always the fresh produce section in your local supermarket. Just be extra sure to wash them thoroughly. This is also important because we cook many of the vegetables with their peels on due to its high nutrient content. Wash all produce, both organic and non-organically grown, to remove any excess soil and remnants from transportation. Use a small amount of dishwashing liquid. There are now some brands that are biodegradable and that have not been tested on animals. You can find these in health food stores and some major chains as well. The brand doesn't really matter, however, as the product will wash off in tap water.

You can use a soft brush or your fingers to loosen debris. Run the surface of the produce under cool running water for a couple of minutes.

Leafy greens, such as spinach, and broccoli should be soaked for five minutes or so before rinsing under tap water. I don't use soap with these leafy types of vegetables, as the soap is hard to remove completely afterwards.

These are some of the vegetables that I use in my recipes:

- broccoli
- carrots
- kelp

- peas
- pumpkin
- squash
- string beans
- sweet potatoes or yams
- zucchini

Some common seasonings you can use include:

- catnip
- dill
- parsley

Here is a list of staples that you should always keep handy in your pantry or refrigerator:

- barley
- cod liver oil
- noodles, elbow macaroni, spaghetti, etc.
- oatmeal, either regular or instant
- unsalted butter
- rice, either brown or white
- salmon oil

With simply a few of these common ingredients you can put together a quick and nutritious meal for your cat in a matter of minutes. In chapter 11 you will find my favorite cat food recipes, and you'll see how easy it is to use your imagination and improvise your own recipes from what you regularly keep handy in your kitchen.

Transitioning to a Home-Cooked Diet

If you have an adult cat that is used to a commercial diet that you would love to introduce to Kitty Grub, you will need to transition them slowly. Your cat will take very little notice of what you are doing to their food.

When beginning the process of changing from commercial to home-cooked, you will begin by introducing a very slight amount of the transition diet (found at the end of this chapter) to the cat's existing feeding routine. Start with as little as half a teaspoon for the first couple of days. This will appear to be the most difficult period, but as time goes by, your cat will begin to get used to the change. By the third week, the amount may be increased by a half a teaspoon.

If you are having a difficult time and your cat is not eating, you can add some mackerel broth to the food. This will ignite a sensory response that will encourage the cat to try the food being offered. Only use this in extremely small amounts, in the form of drops. No more than ten drops is ideal.

Another suggestion is to add some parmesan cheese. It is better to always buy parmesan cheese in blocks—real cheese does not come pre-powdered or shredded. Sprinkle a minimal amount over the food—half a teaspoon at the most. Remember: cats have even fewer taste buds than dogs, so it is their sense of smell that makes them want to eat.

The transition diet should continue for a month if necessary. If your cat absolutely refuses to eat after the first day and the mackerel broth or parmesan additions make no impact, discontinue the home-cooked diet. Cats can immediately develop fatty liver disease, leading to starvation, when deprived of adequate nutrition for more than forty-eight hours. Never starve your cat. If it's not responding to the home-cooked diet, give it what it prefers and consult your vet.

There is no need to supplement while feeding the transition diet, as the commercial cat food you're mixing with the home-cooked food already has sufficient supplementation included.

CHAPTER 10

Case Studies—Home-Cooked Diet Success Stories

Edgar (Juicy Fruit)

E dgar is my second eldest puss. He comes in behind Pooty at thirteen years old. His nickname is Juicy Fruit. I call him that because every time he gets emotional and "kneads dough" on my lap, he drools profusely. It is a sight to see—or feel, as the case may be. He drools that much.

Edgar came into my life, like many of my cats, in a rather tragic way. A friend of mine was in West Virginia at a junkyard looking for what she likes to call treasure. While hunting for goodies, she came across this teeny little black kitten with a white tip on his tail, chewing on a piece of shriveled up lettuce. As pitiful as that sounds, what makes it even more miserable is that it was a freezing, cold day in December.

My friend tried to get in touch with me at the time but was not successful. When she arrived home, she called me again and told me that she had seen this teeny little kitten gnawing on the old shriveled piece of lettuce. She asked me, if she was to go back and get it, would think about fostering it? I responded that if she was willing to go back and retrieve him then I would do better than that—I would actually adopt him. So she went back the next weekend in the hope that he would still be there scrounging for food scraps and that nothing tragic had happened to him.

She had success. When she came to my house to deliver him to me I saw what a miserable little kitten he really was. Not only was his appearance scraggly, but he was obviously in poor health. He was suffering from a severe upper-respiratory infection.

I put him in the bedroom, where, believe it or not, he slept on my pillow for five days straight. My vet put him on a course of antibiotics and I put food and water next to him in the hope that he would respond. He was so incredibly weak he could barely get up to use the cat litter.

In the hope that he would respond to some good food, I started to give him chicken liver and rolled oats. It worked, and he began to get better after the fifth day. Despite this progress, he still didn't leave my room till a full month later.

As he began to heal and his healthy diet was maintained, his coat got so shiny and healthy looking, I felt relieved that Edgar was on the road to recovery. He was becoming so healthy, in fact, that his juices really started flowing. That was when I first noticed how extreme his drool was. I like to think that was his way of showing his love and appreciation for what I had done to help him get better. He simply could not hold it in.

Honey

Honey is a black and white medium-haired tuxedo kitty with white whiskers and an odd stride to his walk. I think he walks like a hoodlum. He's got this weird hunch to him, like a butch-kitty looking for trouble.

Honey, again, like so many of my cats, was a death-row cat from the local shelter. After experiencing firsthand his hobo-like tendencies, I think I know why he ended up there. It hadn't been long since Honey had arrived at my house until he got in trouble again. Honey went missing.

After being gone already for a day and a half, we started calling for him again, restarting the search. We heard a faint cry from afar, saying in kitty-speak, "Here I am, over here." As we approached the faint and eerie sound, we found Honey lying on a bed of grass with dried blood all over his fur.

As I bent down I saw that there was a dark hole near his shoulder. It looked to me as if Honey had been shot. Amazingly, he wasn't dead. He wasn't in great shape, obviously, but at least he was still alive. I'm sure whoever had done this to Honey must have been an angry neighbor. Either that or someone was getting their kicks from shooting at any defenseless creature within range running about in the woods. Honey loved to hunt birds. I wonder if Honey's bird hunting led him into dangerous territory by mistake.

We rushed Honey to the nearest veterinary hospital, where they confirmed that he had taken a bullet. This time, Honey was lucky. His life hung by a thread. The vet there wasn't sure if he could save him. Twenty-four hours, and the inevitable thousands of dollars later, Honey was slowly beginning to show signs of progress. Thank goodness he was recovering.

When we got Honey home he had to be on the proper diet to aid in his healing and recovery. We started him on 80 percent meat protein, but he did not appear to have any kind of appetite. It was crucial that he eat something, or we knew it would be the beginning of the end for Honey, with the pending risk of fatty liver disease and starvation to follow. We began with chicken livers as the primary meat protein for Honey's diet, adding some mackerel and canned salmon to it.

Slowly he started to respond and began to eat, and then after the second day his appetite was back. We knew then that we were really on the road to recovery with Honey. Can you imagine the odds of getting hit by a bullet the way Honey did? And surviving? He's definitely a lucky cat. I am delighted to say that Honey is still around, living it large and stalking birds on my farm like the hoodlum he is.

Cagney Louise and Cooper

Cagney Louise and Cooper were black domestic shorthaired siblings on death row at the local shelter. As I work closely with rescue organizations in the area, including the local shelter, I initially received a call about Cooper. He was three and a half years old and was going to be euthanized within hours. Of course I responded immediately and a friend brought him to me. Cooper seemed healthy and fine and was doing well in one of my spare rooms where there were also other cats that I was currently fostering.

One morning, when I went into the room, I found Cooper coughing and sneezing. I picked him up and discovered that he had thick discharge coming out of every facial orifice. Immediately I rushed him to the veterinarian to be checked over. He had sores all over his lips and tongue. The vet told me it was an upper-respiratory infection and gave me a course of antibiotics to give this ailing puss.

Cooper did not get better. He was misdiagnosed. Sadly for Cooper, he in fact had the deadly calicivirus. The calicivirus is a viral respiratory disease that present its self with sores in the mouth, fever, conjunctivitis, and pneumonia. Combination vaccines include protection against this virus and I know Cooper had been vaccinated at some point. But for whatever reason, his immune system had been compromised. Perhaps the stress of being given up by his owner and ending up at the shelter triggered his immune system into a downward spiral. Cooper declined in health even when I was tube feeding him. When he died, I looked at his give-up paperwork from the shelter and discovered that he had a sister given up with him.

I searched until I found her. She was also on the waitlist to be euthanized. I brought her home, expecting for her to also become sick, since both cats had suffered through the exact same situation and stresses. If she was going to end up like Cooper, I reasoned that at least let her be in a comfortable environment surrounded by care and love, rather than in a sterile shelter environment where her identity is recorded simply as a number.

Strangely, she did not get sick. Cagney Louise had a completely different personality, or "puss-inality" to Cooper. Where Cooper was more introverted and subdued, Cagney was little Miss Personality, carefree in her attitude. The world could have been ending and she would probably care less.

The only thing she really does care (a little too much?) about, is her food. She enjoys being a fuller figured feline, and is proud of her "whatever" with the world attitude. She may be basking out on the bench outside, and a mouse may come right up on her. Cagney would probably open an eyelid (just one—two may expend way too much energy) and register it but decide she gets her food for free so why bother with the effort. She's that laid back.

I suppose that's why she didn't get sick like Cooper. With her non-frail constitution and her super carefree disposition sustaining a strong immune system, the calicivirus passed on her while it attacked her brother.

In memory of her brother Cooper, I decided to keep Cagney.

Cheeba

The day I got the call about this little black and white cat, I knew he was the puss for me. A friend who does rescue work in Baltimore called and said that she'd had no luck in placing this young kitty. He'd been adopted out twice previously and been brought back for various reasons. She called in a personal favor and asked if I would adopt him as it was obvious he did not stand a chance of ever finding the perfect forever home where he was.

When I went to pick him up, I didn't know what I was going to call him. He just seemed like this skinny black and white kitty, with one clouded blind eye. Cheeba had quite the history. My friend told me that a homeless man had rescued Cheeba and his sister from a burning warehouse building. Apparently, he'd heard the desperate cries of these helpless kittens in the building. He rushed into the blazing warehouse to see what the sound was, and he found these two tiny week-old kittens. That homeless man was my hero, as he did what many of us wouldn't do. He grabbed them and ran out of the burning building. Too bad not all people have that kind of courage.

At their immediate veterinary check-up Cheeba and his sister were both found to have terrible upper-respiratory infections, and the vet feared that neither would make it. The vet had to sew both kittens' eyes shut due to the terrible eye infections in so that the eyes could heal themselves. The stitches were later removed in the hope of revealing the eyes both healed. Sadly for Cheeba, he lost the sight in one of his eyes to the infections, but his sister recovered fully.

I knew then that Cheeba was the cat for me, having survived a horrific fire, having recovered from such a severe upper-respiratory infection, and having been rejected twice already from previous adoptions.

When I brought Cheeba home from the vet later that night I noticed that he tentatively approached Pooty and Edgar, then hissed at both of them. Then he went into a corner and huddled there, essentially going into hiding for a couple of days.

Slowly he acclimated to the household. While I was searching for a good name for him, one day I proceeded to pick him up while his back end was pointing in the direction of my chest. I guess his body was a little hyper-reactive due to his recent trauma, as out of the blue, his anal glands ejected, squirting a yellow cheesy substance onto my blouse. My immediate reaction was to think of a ball of cheese, or Cheese Ball. Abbreviated, it became Cheeba.

As Cheeba's diet consisted only of dry food prior to coming to my house, when I would feed my other cats he would sniff at it curiously, as if trying to figure out what it was. Reared solely on commercial food, he was simply unable to fathom a different form of food. I started him on the transition diet slowly, and within the month he was completely weaned off the commercial food.

Thirteen years later he's still going strong and happy and sweet as ever. I realize how lucky I was to have gotten the call to discover the joy of this special puss.

Grandpa Charlie

Grandpa Charlie, as we called him, was a really, really old cat. He'd been brought to the shelter to be euthanized because his owners were moving. They had decided it was not worth taking Charlie, because he was so old, blind in one eye with missing teeth and fur basically gone on half his body. When I got him he was in this pitiful state, but he also had such a chronic upper-respiratory infection that copious amounts of green and yellow mucus were coming out of his nostrils. He would sneeze at least thirty times a day, and with each sneeze would come projectile chunks of gunk, smearing walls and whatever else was in their path.

When I brought Charlie in I wondered how in the world would I ever be able to adopt this cat out. Who on earth would be willing to deal with his physical state and subsequent excretions? When I made the appointment with my vet, Leslie Taylor, she explained to me that Charlie had a chronic upper-respiratory infection. A lot of cats pick up infections when they are dumped at the shelter, so this was fairly typical. What wasn't so typical was the severity of Charlie's particular case. She said that he might need to be on periodic steroids and antibiotics for the rest of his life as his immune system was just so poor. He would probably live with this condition for the rest of his life.

However, with proper care that included love and attention and medication to deal with his health issues, Charlie started feeling better day by day. The proper diet also helped which was rich in meat protein, at a high 90 percent proportion. This would allow for increased bioavailability, a major change from his commercial diet. This meant he was getting real protein, in its purest form, to aid in his recovery and to rebuild his damaged body functions.

Charlie's fur began to grow back in a matter of about a month and a half, and his one good eye became much clearer. Although the upper respiratory infection never went completely away and the periodic use of antibiotics and steroids were needed for him, there is a happy ending to the Charlie tale.

A friend of mine was volunteering for me one day and asked about adopting Charlie. She'd become very attached to him and had been aware of his story from the beginning. After clarifying with her that she really meant my Grandpa Charlie, she said that she wanted to adopt him, as she had managed to fall in love with the sweet, gentle old puss.

I explained clearly his condition and his chronic problems and what taking care of him long term would realistically entail. I made it clear that, as his new owner, frequent vet visits would be in order for the rest of his life. She seemed perfectly okay with it and decided to take Charlie, and the responsibilities that went with him, on.

Months later, when I visited my friend at her home, I caught up with Charlie. He appeared to be in fresh bloom, as if he had rejuvenated his life. Despite his overall improved health and wellbeing, my friend did say that there were marks of Charlie's mucus explosions all over the place, but her life was so much richer for having that sweet old puss in it.

Thumbelina and Brother

Thumbelina and her brother, who, imaginatively, I'd named Brother, were enormously fat cats. I pulled Thumbelina's brother out of the shelter first, but I could not get her out at the same time as she'd bitten someone working there. This had unfortunately happened when someone had tried to pick her up. In obvious discomfort, Thumbelina had struck out at the person who'd created this source of pain and discomfort for her. She had to be in quarantine for ten days, and so, while I waited out her time, I wasted no time in pulling out her brother. Pitifully, Thumbelina's quarantine quarters were restricted to a closet within the shelter's building. As I'm sure you are aware, shelter facilities are ridiculously overextended and unfortunately space is limited, so Thumbelina's exile turned out to be a closet.

Brother had (as predicted) an upper respiratory infection when I brought him home, which he had contracted during his time at the shelter. He proceeded to get worse, even needing to go on and extreme course of antibiotics. Sadly for Brother his health deteriorated dramatically and we had no choice but to put him down. Bizarrely, after finally getting Thumbelina and taking care of her in my home, she did not have the same severity of the infection that Brother did.

We never really had the same health issues for Thumbelina that Brother did. Aside from her obesity, her health was essentially in pretty good order. Currently, Thumbelina is thriving on the proper diet, and what a difference some good food makes.

Steadily, she has lost a good amount of weight. Since I didn't want her to lose weight drastically, even now she continues to be on the transition diet. The course of the transition diet will be longer for her, because she is an obese cat. If she was to lose weight at an extreme rate, it would be a complete shock to her system, triggering drastic health issues.

Thumbelina continues to be in my care, eating well but sensibly, and awaits the perfect forever home.

Sam, Darth Vader's Feline Cousin

Sam was an orange and white tabby, a sweet-natured little man who was brought to me by one of my dearest friends. He'd been living his life outdoors at an antique market, banned from ever accessing the inside of the building there, even in the coldest of winter.

Sam was FIV positive (feline immunodeficiency virus), the kitty equivalent of AIDS. He was also blind in one eye and had scar tissue over the eyeball, which made it appear cloudy and obscured. In addition, Sam had scar tissue in his nasal passage, perhaps due to chronic upper respiratory infections or possibly some kind of severe blunt trauma, such as being hit by a car. This made Sam appear as if he had a pig nose, as if it had been pushed up and in.

This was not just superficial damage for Sam. Due to the structural damage of his nasal passages, his breathing was very loud and heavy, like that of Darth Vader. It would sound like a gurgle, rattling and labored. You knew when Sam walked into the room— you'd hear him before you'd see him. He'd snore so badly at night he would keep you awake. But this sweet boy had the best personality.

He would come on trail walks with my dogs and me on my property, no matter how long or far we'd go. Sam thrived on the closeness of being bonded to somebody. He loved company, and would always look interested, even if you were just sitting sipping a cup of tea.

He also thrived on the healthy wholesome diet that I provided for him. I believe this was a major factor in prolonging his life, as he lived with his FIV for longer than anyone had ever expected. In my honest opinion, if it were not for the proper nourishment he received once he came into my care, he would not have lived a fraction of what he did.

His diet consisted almost every day of chicken livers in combination with other proteins. I prepared his food in this way not just because he liked them, but also because they were rich in every vitamin that he needed to maintain optimum health. Due to his compromised immune system, Sam was very susceptible to picking up any infection. Nevertheless, he lived a very full and active life and was not deprived of a natural outdoor environment. He thrived for many years with me and finally succumbed to an upper respiratory infection. He lives in my heart and in my memories every day.

Spider

Spider is a black cat that looks like what you might imagine an Egyptian kitty to look like. I first saw her at the shelter when I was there picking up another cat for fostering. Sadly, the plight of all black cats (and dogs for that matter) is that they are the least adopted kind of cat at shelters. The reason for this may well be superstition, or possibly poor showings in their cages. However, in my opinion, black cats are the most beautiful cat due to the fact that their sleek monotone appearance allows for the true nature of their soul to shine through their eyes. All too often they are overlooked for more fluffy, visually interesting, colorful cats.

Spider is the coolest kitty in the world. I named her Spider because she is long and lean and stealthy, like a hairy black spider. When she sits next to Cagney, my other black cat, Spider looks like a supermodel. (As you read above, Cagney is my plus-sized model.)

Spider is young, about a year old. I think that because I rescued her so early in her life she was able to develop and maximize her natural hunting tendencies. When provided with the perfect hunting environment, she has shown her natural predatory finesse.

Spider's specialty is bat hunting. This got her into a whole lot of trouble with me when I first found a dead bat in my bathroom. Aside from feeling a little grossed out, I also had to think practically. I sent the bat off to be tested for rabies, which thankfully came back negative.

Now I frequently find dead bats around the property, and I know it is Spider's handiwork. I know that she does not eat the bats, not even the heads. She just likes to catch them while they're flying. She does it simply for the sport of exercising her natural hunting instincts.

She is like no other cat I have ever encountered. Spider is the best little huntress on the farm and her physique shows it. Her coat and her health prove that eating bugs and small animals is a necessity for complete health. Physically she is not like any other domesticated cat that I have seen. She is so aerodynamic in her extreme physical abilities and will eat anything I put I front of her. Remember, earlier I said that all cats by nature are good eaters. So Spider, being almost original wildcat in my view, is the perfect example of that.

CHAPTER 11

Kitty Grub Recipes

The following Kitty Grub recipes are extensions of any basic recipe format. They offer ample opportunities for variation and experimentation. Once you have mastered these, you'll be surprised at how inventive you become after a very short time. When you see how responsive your cats will be, you'll probably surprise yourself at how eager you are to experiment with different ingredients in order to find the recipes your cat loves best.

The ingredients listed in these recipes are for single-serving portions. The specific amounts of each ingredient are in their *cooked* state. Remember it is better to overcook amounts—the cat will leave what it doesn't eat. If you prefer to cook bulk quantities (which is how I typically cook, and in my opinion is the easiest way to do it), multiply the amount by the days to be covered. Usually, as a general approximation, I take a combination of a couple of 3–5 lb trays of meat, cook it with a pound of combined vegetables and about the same of the grain, and that lasts the week.

One thing to note is that food offered to your puss should never be cold, straight from the fridge. Serving the food at room temperature is ideal. Often, to take the chill off, I'll pop my cats' food bowls into the microwave for a few seconds. This also releases some of the juices that have congealed in their chilled state. Just make sure you don't leave the food in there for too long or else it will get too hot!

These recipes are the ones I prepare most often for my own cats, and the most popular ordered by cat food clients. As you'll come to discover, there is nothing difficult about my recipes. They have a wide margin for error and adaptation. Most importantly have fun with them, and remember that your beloved puss will not only enjoy the "real" food but will be much better off health-wise in the long run.

Broths

At the beginning of most of my recipes you will be asked to brown, boil, or stew your meat and boil your vegetables. Broth is the liquid reserved from the boiling process. This broth may be added to main dishes as a final seasoning or used to replace the water when preparing rice or pasta. The broth becomes a source of additional protein, vitamins, and minerals.

CHICKEN OR TURKEY BROTH

Follow this recipe for chicken or turkey broth when you make your general recipes.

- 1 ½ cups cubed chicken
  - or 1 ½ cups ground turkey
  - or 1 ½ cups chopped chicken hearts and livers (12 oz)
- 2 ½ cups water

Boil the chicken or chicken parts in water for about 45 minutes, the ground turkey for 30 minutes. Strain the meat from your liquid and refrigerate for use in your other recipes. Reserve the broth in an airtight plastic container in the freezer, or keep it in the refrigerator, where it will stay fresh for three to four days.

When the broth is cooled, it will become gelatinous, which actually makes it easy to spoon and measure. Yet it thaws and liquefies rapidly when spooned over heated ingredients.

BEEF OR LAMB BROTH

Follow this recipe for beef or lamb broth when you make your general recipes.

- 1 ½ cups ground or cubed beef
  - or: 1 ½ cups ground or cubed lamb
- 2 ½ cups water

Boil the ground beef or lamb in water for about 30 minutes, the cubed meat for 45 minutes, until tender. Strain the meat from your liquid and refrigerate for use in your other recipes. Reserve the broth in an airtight plastic container in the freezer, or keep it in the refrigerator.

When the broth is cooled, it will become gelatinous, which actually makes it easy to spoon and measure. Yet it thaws and liquefies rapidly when spooned over heated ingredients.

VEGETABLE BROTH

Whenever you boil vegetables for your main dishes, save the cooking water—that's a vegetable broth. Vegetable broths can add nutrients to your recipes when they are substituted for plain water.

Some vegetables, such as beets, produce very aromatic and colorful broths. Beet broth looks like red wine. If you use vegetable broth for cooking rice, it becomes truly beautiful.

To create a vegetable broth, strain out the vegetable pulp after boiling (otherwise what you've got is soup) and store in the refrigerator for future recipes.

Supplements

Adding any supplements to each dish should be done just before serving the meal. When in doubt about how much to supplement, remember: about a dash is okay. Suggested supplements include clam juice, salt, cod liver oil—calcium powder.

Please also remember: do not supplement any meals if you are also feeding a commercial cat food diet of any kind in combination with your home-cooked food. These have adequate supplements as part of their ingredient mix.

Eggshell Powder

Eggshell powder is the absolute best source of calcium around. Making it is also a great way to not waste raw materials. If you eat eggs or cook with eggs, toss the empty shells in a clean plastic container until you are ready to make another big batch.

Sterilize twelve or more shells by baking them on a tray in the oven for 15 to 20 minutes at 350 degrees. Grind them finely—an electric coffee-bean grinder is perfect, or you can use a mortar and pestle—and save the eggshell powder in your refrigerator. If the powder is kept cool and dry, it should maintain for quite a long time (throw it out if it starts to change color or appear moldy). If you don't want to use eggshells, you can always try bone meal instead.

DAILY CALCIUM SUPPLEMENT

If you have a single eggshell left over from breakfast, use it to make a daily calcium supplement that it appropriate for cats transitioning to supplements, as well as those with any yeast allergies.

- 1 eggshell, finely ground
- 1 tablespoon cod liver oil

- 1 teaspoon kelp or chelated seaweed powder

Boil an eggshell for five minutes and then grind it to a powder. Again, you can use the small coffee-bean grinder, or do it by hand. The shell should be as fine as possible. You can also purchase ground eggshells from a health food store, but homemade powder is better.

Add the cod liver oil and kelp or chelated seaweed powder, and combine thoroughly in a small mixing bowl.

To serve, add a small pinch of the mixture to your cat's fresh food.

BASIC RECIPES

CARNIVORE'S DELIGHT

1 ½ cups chicken livers
¼ cup rolled oats
2 T cooked carrot
2 T cooked squash
2 T salmon broth
1 T unsalted butter

Sear the chicken livers in a skillet for about one minute each side. Bring a cup of water to boil, adding a pinch of salt. Add rolled oats and cook about two and a half minutes until mushy. Boil vegetables also until mushy. Drain—do not throw away vegetable broth. Let cool. Put all ingredients together in a bowl and incorporate well, adding the salmon broth to mix. Allow to cool to room temperature, then serve.

FERAL CAT SPECIAL

Cats love this recipe, due to the smell of the salmon broth—it brings out their feral side!

1 ½ cups chicken liver
¼ cup rolled oats
¼ cup cooked white rice
2 T salmon broth
1 T unsalted butter

Sear the chicken livers in a skillet with the butter for about two minutes each side. Bring a cup of water to boil, adding a pinch of salt. Add rolled oats and cook about two and a half minutes until mushy. Boil rice also until mushy. Let cool. Put all ingredients together in a bowl and incorporate well, adding the salmon broth to mix. Allow to cool to room temperature, then serve.

HALLOWEEN 'SAM HEIN' MIDNIGHT SPECIAL

1 ½ cups ground chicken
¼ cup cooked pumpkin
¼ cup cooked green peas
2 T unsalted butter

Brown the chicken in the butter in a large skillet. Stir frequently, and do not overcook. Boil vegetables until mushy. Let cool. Put all ingredients together in a bowl and incorporate well. Allow to cool to room temperature, then serve.

THANKSGIVING DINNER

1 ½ cups cubed or ground turkey
¼ cup cooked string beans
¼ cup cooked sweet potato
1 T unsalted butter

Brown the turkey in the butter in a large skillet over a low heat for about thirty minutes or so. Do not overcook. Boil string beans until tender, sloe to mushy. Boil the sweet potato and mash. Put all ingredients together in a bowl and incorporate well. Allow to cool to room temperature, then serve.

BEEF AND EGG DINNER

1 ½ cups ground beef
1 egg
2 T cooked celery
2 T unsalted butter
1 t catnip (fresh or dried)

In a large skillet add the butter then brown the ground beef. Add the egg and mix well through meat. Stir frequently for about ten minutes. Do not overcook. Bring a small pot of water to boil, adding the celery. Overcook until mushy. Place all ingredients together in a bowl, including the catnip. Stir well. Cool to room temperature, then serve.

ASIAN FUSION

1 ½ cups cubed chicken
2 T cooked white rice
¼ cup cooked grated carrot
2 T cooked green peas
2 T unsalted butter

Brown the chicken with the butter in a large skillet over low heat for about ten minutes. Conserve the broth. Bring water to a boil, adding the white rice. Overcook until mushy. Boil the carrots and the peas also until mushy. Drain and let cool. Put all ingredients together in a bowl and incorporate well, adding the chicken broth to mix. Serve at room temperature.

AN EGGY FEAST

3 large eggs
2 T cooked sweet potato
2 T cooked yellow squash
1 T salmon broth
1 t parsley (chopped and steamed)
2 T unsalted butter

Beat the eggs with a fork making sure the egg yolks and egg whites are thoroughly mixed. Grease a small skillet with the butter and pour the eggs into it. Scramble the eggs over a low heat, stirring continuously until cooked through—about five minutes. Boil sweet potato and yellow squash, cooking until mushy. Put all ingredients together in a bowl and incorporate well, adding the salmon broth and parsley to mix. Allow to cool to room temperature, then serve.

A FISHY DISH

1 ½ cups shredded smoked salmon
1 large egg
3 T cooked brown rice
2 T cooked asparagus or green peas

Hard boil the egg. Remove shell and mash well when cooled. Overcook brown rice, boiling until mushy. Also over cook the asparagus or green peas until soft, then mash when cooled. Put all cooked ingredients together in a bowl with the smoked salmon and incorporate well. Serve at room temperature.

CHICKEN AND RICE AND ALL THINGS NICE

1 ½ cups chicken thigh meat (skin on)
¼ cup cooked carrots
2 T cooked green peas
2 T cooked white rice

Stew the chicken thighs with their skins on in a pot of water for about forty minutes. Drain, allow to cool, then remove the thigh bones. Overcook the white rice until mushy. Boil vegetables also until mushy. Let cool. Put all ingredients together in a bowl and incorporate well. Serve at room temperature.

POOTY POOT

This recipe is named after Princess Pooty, as it is one of her favorite dishes.

1 ½ cups ground turkey
3 T rolled oats
3 T cooked squash
Dash of grated parmesan cheese
2 T unsalted butter

Brown the turkey in a skillet with the butter. Boil a cup of water in a small pot and add rolled oats. Cook about two and a half minutes until mushy. Drain and set aside. Boil squash also until mushy. Let cool. Put all ingredients together in a bowl and incorporate well, adding the grated parmesan cheese to mix. Serve at room temperature.

Healing Recipes

Food has the incredible healing power to maintain and restore health. It fuels every physiological system and is therefore the body's closest ally in the prevention of and recovery from disease. This is also why poor diet can, over time, lead to disastrous consequences. When a cat is not receiving the required vitamins, minerals, and other essential nutrients, there may be a downward spiraling effect of lowered immunity followed by ill health.

Preventing physical ailments is not always easy, and different cats have different susceptibilities to disease. Since your beloved puss is dependent on you, it is worth educating yourself on the best way to help. One place to start learning is the Internet, which is a great source of the most up-to-date information and research in cat nutrition and overall wellbeing.

The following recipes are suggested for specific health issues as well as general ailments in your cat. Remember, as with all my recipes, nothing is set in stone as far as ingredients and specific amounts are concerned. Be flexible and experiment with whatever works best for your puss.

You'll notice that there are no grains included in nearly all of the healing recipes. The proportions here are 90 percent protein, with the remaining 10 percent made up of vegetables. As increased protein is needed for optimum healing, the grains have been omitted. Carbohydrates are provided through the vegetables.

HEALING RECIPES

ANTI-CANCER FOOD

The tomato juice in this recipe is a great antioxidant and an excellent source of vitamin C.

1 ½ cups chopped/cubed lamb
1 T green beans (extra mushy)
1 T pureed squash
1 T cottage cheese
1 T tomato juice
1 T cod liver oil

Sear cubed lamb in a skillet for about seven minutes. Let cool. Fully cook the squash and the green beans until both are mushy. They should easily mush with a wooden spoon, but you can throw them in the food processor if needed. When fully cooled, put all ingredients into a bowl, including the cottage cheese and tomato juice. Mix very well. Before serving add the flaxseed oil. Serve at room temperature.

WEIGHT LOSS WONDER

Even though this is a weight loss recipe, it is important to keep the skin on the chicken. Remember: fat burns fat.

2 chicken thighs (skin on)
2 T butter
1 T broccoli (mashed)
1 T carrot (mashed)

Stew the chicken thighs with the skins on for about forty minutes. Remove the thighbone once cooked and cooled. Overcook the broccoli and the carrots and mash both. Add all ingredients together in a mixing bowl, including the butter. Serve at room temperature.

ANEMIA A-NO-MORE FOOD

Livers are full of iron, as is spinach, a necessary element in any diet helping to aid anemia.

1 ½ cups chicken livers
¼ cup chicken hearts (chopped)
2 T overcooked white rice
1 T cooked spinach
2 T unsalted butter

Sear the chicken livers and hearts in the butter in a skillet for about seven minutes. Add the cooked spinach and continue to cook a further minute. Overcook the white rice, then combine all ingredients in a mixing bowl. Mix very well. Let cool, then serve at room temperature.

KIDNEY HEALING MEAL

3 eggs
¼ cup liver
¼ cup zucchini
1 T parsley (chopped finely and steamed)
1 T cottage cheese

Hard boil the eggs, then remove shells. When completely cooled, mashed the eggs very well (or puree in food processor). Fully cook the zucchini until mushy—save the broth! When all ingredients are fully cooled, put into a mixing bowl, then add the vegetable broth, the parsley, and the cottage cheese. Note: although flaxseed oil is really not used for cats, it is important to note that flaxseed oil has been proven to help the to clean the glomeruli which are the filtering unit of the kidney. So I leave it to you to decide if you would like to use it or not.

Non-Meat Protein Diet

3 eggs
1 T cooked rolled oats
1 T vegetable broth
1 T cottage cheese
1 T cod liver oil
2 T unsalted butter
A dash of salt

Hard boil the eggs, then remove shells. When completely cooled, mash the eggs very well (or puree in food processor). Cook the rolled oats well—at least two and a half minutes. When cooled, place in mixing bowl with eggs then add the vegetable broth, butter and the cottage cheese. Mix very well. Before serving add the cod liver oil. Serve at room temperature.

Anti-IBD Meal

For inflammatory bowel disorders. Depending on what your cat is sensitive to nutritionally, you can adjust this recipe from rolled oats to white rice or even no grains at all. You can also change the protein if that becomes a source of irritation to your cat's digestive system. This is Edgar's favorite recipe. As a long-term sufferer of IBD, he does really well on this meal.

1 ¾ cups ground lamb
2 T sweet potato (cooked and mashed)
2 T rolled oats (cooked and mushy)
A dash of salt

Braise the ground lamb in a skillet, stirring frequently. Do not overcook—five minutes is probably sufficient. Boil the skinned sweet potato until soft then mash it up. Do the same with the rolled oats: about two and a half minutes should be plenty of cooking time. Put altogether into a mixing bowl and add the salt. When all ingredients are cooled to room temperature, serve.

DIABETES DIET

In this recipe I use red lentils because they are a great source of protein and are easily digestible. If you are considering adding a grain to your diabetes recipe, please be aware that you must use only rolled oats or steel cut oats. This is because oats do not convert to sugar immediately—they take some time to digest.

1 ¾ cups cubed turkey
2 T green beans
2 T cooked red lentils

Boil the lentils in water for about thirty minutes or until extra mushy. Fully cook the green beans until mushy. Stew the turkey for about twenty minutes until cooked through. Drain well. Put all ingredients into a mixing bowl, and blend together well. Let cool, then serve at room temperature.

HEALING HEART RECIPE

Chicken hearts are full of taurine—a great source of one of the eleven essential amino acids in a cat's daily diet.

1 ¾ cups chicken hearts (chopped)
2 T barley
2 T green peas

Braise the chopped chicken hearts in a skillet for about three minutes. Fully cook the green peas until mushy. Boil the barley, overcooking it until it can also be mashed or pureed. Put all ingredients together in a mixing bowl, then blend well. Allow to cool before serving at room temperature.

UTI SPECIAL

For cats suffering with urinary tract issues. Remember that tomatoes are a great source of vitamin C and a wonderful antioxidant. If your cat has a specific kind of crystals, it is important to know exactly which kind so the recipe can be adjusted accordingly. The pH balance in the cat's body determines what kind of crystals will develop. Some foods, such as tomatoes, can prove too acidic, so they will need to be exchanged for something else.

1 ¾ cups cubed chicken
2 T cooked white rice
1 T yellow squash
2 T chicken broth
1 T cooked tomatoes
1 T chicken fat

Sear the chicken with the skin for about ten minutes. Fully cook the white rice, the tomatoes, and the yellow squash until all are mushy. Place all ingredients together in a mixing bowl, then add the chicken fat and the broth. Mix well. Let cool, then serve at room temperature.

Resources

The organizations, publications, and websites listed below are resources intended to assist you in caring for your cat. I would love to hear from you, so I begin with my own:

Barker's Grub
Dickerson, MD
Ph. (301) 349-0808
Email: barkingholler@yahoo.com

VETERINARY MEDICINE

Academy of Veterinary Homeopathy
751 NE 168th Street
North Miami Beach, FL 33162-2427
(305) 653-7244
www.acadvethom.com

International Association of Veterinary Homeopathy
334 Knollwood Lane
Woodstock, GA 30188
(770) 516-5954

American Holistic Veterinary Medical Association
2214 Old Emmorton Road
Bel Air, MD 21015
(410) 569-2346
Email: AHVMA@compuserve.com
You can contact this organization to find the name of a holistic veterinarian in your area.

American Academy of Veterinary Acupuncture
PO Box 419
Hygiene, CO 80533 -0419
(305) 653-7244
http://aava.org

Animal Chiropractic Center
623 Main Street
Hillsdale, IL 61257
(309) 658-2622

Ani-Med Phone Information Service (ASPCA)
(888) 252-7381 (toll free)
Here you can get recorded information on wide-ranging cat-care topics.

American Animal Hospital Association
(800) 883-6301 (toll free)
www.healthypet.com
Established in 1933, this is an organization of more than 17,000 veterinary care providers, which can help you locate an emergency medical center in a crisis.

Herbs & Flower Essences

Equilite, Inc.
Ardsley, NY
(800) 942-LYTE (toll free)
(914) 693-2553
This business custom makes herbal remedies and flower essences for cats and dogs with behavioral disorders.

Nelson Bach USA, Inc.
Wilmington, MA
(800) 319-9151 (toll free)
(978) 988-3833
This business makes the famous Bach flower essences, of which Rescue Remedy is especially handy.

Flower Essences Service
Nevada City, CA
(800) 548-0075 (toll free)
(530) 265-0258

Rescue Groups

American Society for the Prevention of Cruelty to Animals
424 East 92nd Street
New York, NY 10128-6804
(212) 876-7700
www.aspca.org
Founded in 1866, the ASPCA was the first humane organization in the Western hemisphere. To find your national chapter go to their web site or check your local yellow pages. The website has links to organizations in every state.

Humane Society of the United States
National Headquarters
2100 L Street, NW
Washington, DC 20007
(202)452-1100
www.hsus.org

ANIMAL SHELTERS

The easiest place to locate your nearest animal shelter is by checking in your phone book, or looking online. Public animal control and care facilities are often listed under the city or county health department or police department.

Save Our Strays
www.saveourstrays.com
A website with links to many others, including those in your local area.

Cyber Pet–Rescue
www.cyberpet.com
A website full of useful articles and links about cats.

Metro Pets Online
www.metropets.org
(301) 490-5266
This Maryland-based organization helps people find the right cat for them, as well as other useful links.

Recommended Reading

Lewis, Lon D., Mark Morris, Jr., and Michael S. Hand. *Small Animal Clinical Nutrition, III.* Topeka, KS: Mark Morris Associates, 1987.

Pitcairn, Richard H., and Susan Hubble Pitcairn. *Dr. Pitcairn's Complete Guide to Natural Health for Cats and Dogs.* Emmaus, PA: Rodale Press, 1995.

Schoen, Alan, and Pam Proctor. *Love, Miracles, and Animal Healing.* New York: Fireside, 1996.

Printed in the United States
By Bookmasters